LINCOLN
FREES THE SLAVES

Reproduced by courtesy of Amos Pinchot, Esq.

ABRAHAM LINCOLN

(At the time of the Douglas debates)

LINCOLN
FREES THE SLAVES

BY

STEPHEN LEACOCK

ILLUSTRATED

G·P·PUTNAM'S SONS
NEW YORK
MCMXXXIV

MANUFACTURED
IN THE UNITED STATES OF AMERICA
AT THE VAN REES PRESS

CONTENTS

CHAPTER   PAGE

I. SLAVERY IN AMERICA 13

II. THE IRREPRESSIBLE CONFLICT 33

III. LINCOLN IN ILLINOIS 51

IV. TOWARDS THE ABYSS 84

V. SECESSION 107

VI. WAR 126

VII. EMANCIPATION 149

VIII. EPILOGUE 161

APPENDIX—FINAL EMANCIPATION PROCLAMATION 171

INDEX 173

ILLUSTRATIONS

ABRAHAM LINCOLN . . . . *Frontispiece*
  (At the time of the Douglas debates)
  Reproduced by courtesy of Amos Pinchot, Esq.

                                                    PAGE
WHAT WILL HE DO WITH THEM? 53
  (From *Vanity Fair*, October, 1862)

SCENE FROM THE AMERICAN TEMPEST 77
  (From *Punch*, January, 1863)

AN HEIR TO THE THRONE, OR THE NEXT REPUBLICAN
  CANDIDATE 103
  (A Currier and Ives print of 1860)

CONTRABANDS COMING INTO THE UNION LINES . . . 137
  (A contemporary drawing by Thomas Nast in *Harper's
    Weekly*, 1863)

LINCOLN'S FIRST READING OF THE PROCLAMATION TO
  HIS CABINET 155
  (From a contemporary engraving)

LINCOLN ENTERING RICHMOND, APRIL 3, 1865 . . . 165
  (From a contemporary engraving)

PRESIDENT LINCOLN'S FUNERAL PROCESSION 169
  (From *Harper's Weekly*, May, 1865)

LINCOLN
FREES THE SLAVES

I

SLAVERY IN AMERICA

LOOKING back on it, the existence of slavery
seems one of the great facts, one of the domi-
nating factors, in the history of America. In
retrospect it looms large. But to the people of the
time—at least until it had almost run its course—it
did not seem a large fact or a particularly important
fact at all. It was just part of life as they knew it.
It was to them as poverty is to us. Those of us who
are not poor, seldom think about it, and even the
poor take it largely for granted. But if the time ever
comes when poverty is eliminated, its existence will
seem, to those who look back upon us, the great central fact of our history;—not our wars, our science,
our machinery, our art, but the existence amongst
us of poverty, of the slums, of people born into want
and dying in penury. How we could have tolerated
it, will seem a mystery to a generation that no longer
has to do so. Why did not our hearts burn within
us at the thought of it? The historian will record the
peculiar callousness of our generation towards the
suffering of the poor, and misinterpret it in our dis-
favor.

But such callousness to what we cannot change is
the price at which we live. If we each tasted the

sharp agony of others' sorrows we could not long survive.

So with slavery in the past. Generations of people were born and died in America and gave no more thought to slavery than we do to poverty,—as much and as little

Slavery had come down through the ages as part of the world's history. There were slaves in the ancient world. The Greeks and Romans looked upon human suffering, at large and in the persons of those not dear to them, with cold neutrality. Students of classical literature will look in vain for tears shed over the slaves broken in the galley, over the slave gangs that built the pyramids beneath the lash, or over the cruel deaths in the arena. If Lucretius could write "the world is full of weeping" (*sunt lachrymæ rerum*) he meant it in a large philosophic sense in which it became a pleasure to contemplate it. Nor had Christianity ever condemned slavery. It opened for the slave the larger freedom of the Kingdom of Heaven. With that hope, the chains became an opportunity; "Slaves, obey your masters," so ran the text (mistranslated into "servants" in King James's time, to make it apply to footmen and gamekeepers in a nation that had no Africans).

Slavery was, so to speak, a part of human thought. The kindly Thomas More writing of a *Utopia*, full of light and happiness, put slaves into it,—the slave being a sort of ticket-of-leave man rescued from crime and singing in the kitchen.

Thus slavery was a part of life and, for those who must perforce think of it, the whole of life could be explained away as a vale of tears.

14

Slavery, it is true, had died out in Europe between the days of Rome and the time of Christopher Columbus. But there had been no condemnation of it and no legislation against it. It had not died out for moral reasons but from the simple fact that it had ceased to "pay." The existence of slavery, indeed, is closely circumscribed in the economic sense. It can exist where great masses of men can be forced to a simple uniform task. Slaves built the pyramids. It can exist where the torrid heat of the climate and the enervating atmosphere undermine the energy of the individual man: where the soil can be tilled with driven labor, beaten to its task, brainless and without hope: or it can exist as an appanage of the tyranny of the palace or as a luxury of domestic life where subservience is more valued than efficiency. But as civilization advances slavery retreats. The task becomes too complicated for driven brains and beaten bodies. This is all the more so in a diversified and varied country, with never a wood or field exactly like another and where an invigorating climate stimulates mechanical genius. Here, sooner or later, work must depend upon freedom, or on the simulation of it. Looked at broadly, the medieval slave changed to the serf, and the serf to the hired laborer, as a means of keeping him going. By the time of Queen Elizabeth a slave in England would have been of no value,—except as a dusky Pompey in livery, an object rather of pride than of profit.

Slavery, therefore, died out in Europe for economic, not moral, reasons; a fact which made it all the easier for it to come to life again. Hence it came to life again with a rush when the colonization of the New World rendered it again a source of economic profit. There was no prejudice against it. When Queen Elizabeth honored the first English slave-catcher by making him Sir John Hawkins, there was no outcry. On the contrary,—the honor fell to him as it would today to any one who re-established an ancient industry.

Not that the people of the Middle Ages were worse, or very much worse, than we are. But they were much more callous to human physical suffering. We stand appalled at their cruel punishments, their dungeons, the savage brutality of their law. But they, if they could know us, would stand appalled at what they would think our crooked mentality, our universal cheating,—in a word, at what we call "business." The honorable knight, or the pious abbot, or even the plain yeoman of the Middle Ages would regard us as a pack of unreliable crooks. No knight would have allowed himself, even if he could have understood the process, to buy International Armour Ltd. in the hope that it would turn out to be worth more than what he paid for it. To pick up for a few shillings, from a poor ignorant shopkeeper, an *antique* which proves to be priceless, would have seemed a hideous piece of dishonesty to a generation which thought nothing of the rack and the "question" and a dungeon sunk below the sunlight.

Underneath it all no doubt is progress, broad and slow and at the end of it, still unseen, is the Kingdom of Heaven on earth.

All the world is familiar with the story of how the nations of Europe, seeking the trade and treasure of the East, stumbled upon the empty continent of America. Slavery only came on the scene as an unforeseen consequence when the era of treasure hunting changed to that of colonial plantation. The first explorers wanted quick results. They wanted trade at the fabulous profits of ivory for beads, or the pillage of junks and temples and treasure houses at a profit higher still. Even when they reached out for the empty continent of America, their first thought was for gold and silver and precious stones. For the inhabitants their only care was to declare them all Christians, thereby saving them in millions, to take away their gold and to carry some of them home as a sort of certificate of discovery.

It is true that the idea of bringing the natives to Europe to make slaves of them did come up as an early incident of discovery. Columbus himself, in his voyage of 1493, in which he had a fleet of seventeen ships, brought home 500 Caribbeans. But Queen Isabella's heart and conscience were troubled at it. The natives were sent back again. In any case there was little market for them in Europe. The Barbary and Algerian pirates used slaves but they caught enough among the Christians. For the other civilized countries the land economy left no place for slavery.

But it was natural that the Europeans should hit upon the system of catching slaves in Africa and taking them to America,—the source of woes unnumbered and still unfinished. The two continents were disclosed at the same time and it was soon found that on the American side of the ocean the natives of the West Indies were too soft, and the North American

Indians too hard, to supply the labor demanded by the whites. The natives of the island paradise found by Columbus died under the lash.

On the mainland of North America the "Indian" proved of no use for the plantations. The red man would not work: he would rather die. The acceptance of death and the scornful tolerance of pain were among the redeeming features of a race whose fiendish delight in cruelty for cruelty's sake forfeited their right to live. Those who know properly the history of such a tribe as the Senecas,—cruel, filthy and cannibal,—will harbor no illusions about the "noble red man." But work the red man would not. The black man will work when he has to, but not otherwise. The white man cannot stop working. Take away his work as a necessity and he brings it back again under the name of "business" or golfs himself to exhaustion.

So it came to be the destiny of America that the whites cleared out the red men, and brought in the black men to work under white direction. Each race fulfilled its seeming destiny.

When the Portuguese discovered the western coast of Africa (1434-1500) they brought back black men to be sold to the Moors and to the Spaniards. This started a trade that was lucrative but limited. With the opening up of America, wider opportunities were presented. Negro slaves were sent out to Hispaniola as early as 1502. King Ferdinand especially ordered consignments of them for the mines. Pious bishops and clerics, such as the famous Las Casas, recommended the import of negroes as a sub-

18

stitute for the Caribbean race, sinking to death under European brutality. Private greed, the world's greatest motive power, thus sheltered itself as usual behind a front of piety. African natives were brought over in thousands and presently in tens of thousands.

It must be understood that slavery did not grow up in the American colonies as the result of a plan. The promoters of the London Company that first permanently established Virginia were not thinking in terms of slave labor and of plantations. Their hope lay elsewhere. The earliest and liveliest was for a discovery of a quick route to the fabled wealth of the Indies. One early explorer carried with him letters addressed to the Khan of Tartary and looked for him up the Chickahominy River. He wasn't there. A second hope was gold. The first returning ship brought to England a cargo of glittering dirt. It wasn't gold. Beyond that was the idea of Indian trade and the easy production of silk and wine. Honest work came last.

The colony was hopelessly mismanaged. Of the first hundred settlers—all men—sixty died in the first year. There was no private land, no incentive to work. Then came tobacco, raised by John Rolfe in 1612. This changed everything. Next came the negroes, a bargain lot of twenty sold to the settlement at large by a Dutch privateer or pirate—in 1619. After that things moved forward. Wiser councils allotted land to the settlers. New people came in every year,—and more negroes. By 1649 there were 15,000 settlers and 300 blacks. The tobacco plantations spread up the rivers, each river an artery of settlement, each plantation a seaport in itself. The tobacco crop ravaged the land, left it as scrub and wilderness, and passed on. But the colony grew constantly. Tobacco held it up. England by this time was smoking seriously. Soon after the restoration of Merry King Charles II, 12,000 tons (50,000 hogsheads) of Virginia and Maryland tobacco went up each year in English pipe smoke. By the year 1671 there were 2,000 negroes in Virginia in a total population of 40,000. What their legal status was no one exactly knew. They were just servants forever. But after the restoration the law called them "slaves," and whatever individual rights they once had disappeared in the slave codes of the Old Dominion of the eighteenth century. A slave was worth about £30 in Governor Berkeley's day. Long-term white convicts sold at about £15. The negro was coming into his own. No doubt it all seemed natural enough at the time.

Slavery slid easily into its place in the rice-growing colonies of the Carolinas. The rice, brought from Madagascar in 1694, was a huge success. Black labor, impervious to heat and damp as the mist itself, was just the thing for it. Slaves were imported in shiploads to the great profit of the Royal African Company, the slave catchers of the day,—as respectable in the England of the eighteenth century as the Johannesburg mines and coolies were in the twentieth. By the middle of Queen Anne's reign the Carolinas contained about 3,500 whites and over 4,000 black slaves. All through the first half of the eighteenth century the blacks outran the whites in number more and more.

Below the Carolinas in 1732 was born the gentle Georgia, the offspring of piety as a refuge for the oppressed, the debtors and the meek. There slavery was forbidden, and there rum was excluded. The noble founder, General James Oglethorpe, was at the same time one of the directors of the Royal African (Slave) Company. To understand this queer inconsistent fact, we must come down British history all the way to Cecil Rhodes.

Under these circumstances the import of negroes from Africa to America became one of the leading features of the world's commerce. British energy shouldered itself into the new trade. It was for a hundred years as respectable as it was profitable. John Hawkins received as the emblem of his knighthood a crest with a negro in chains. When the slave ships came to Virginia the planters eagerly helped themselves. New England, with but little use for slave labor, entered gladly into the trade, a fine stimulus for a maritime coast with ships to build and cargoes to seek. In England the Royal African Company obtained under Charles II a monopoly of the trade in negroes. But under William and Mary (1698) it was thrown open to all British subjects, a broad generous gesture, comparable to the widening of the franchise.

Much humbug and hypocrisy surrounds the history of the British connection with slavery. After it was all over, somebody invented a characteristic song about the British flag, sung at a thousand Victorian pianos which declared:

> *"That fla-ag may float o'er a shot-torn wreck*
> *But never shall float o'er a slave!"*

As a matter of fact the flag probably floated over more slaves than any other flag, or two flags, in the world. British enterprise at sea reached out for the new trade. The Treaty of Utrecht of 1713 contained as one of its triumphs the Assiento clause, carrying over from the Dutch and the French to the British the right to supply 4,800 slaves yearly for thirty years to the Spanish colonies. To that was added an enormous importation into the British colonies themselves. To Jamaica alone over 600,000 negroes were brought during the eighteenth century. Virginia when the colonial days ended contained 200,000 slaves. About 20,000 blacks were brought from Africa each year during the eighteenth century —over 2,000,000 in all. There were nearly 200 British ships engaged in the trade. The British alone had forty depots along the African coast. They shared with the noble commerce of the Hudson Bay the honorable name of "factories"; and what they made, the world has not even yet cast out of its system.

The slave trade is one of the horrors of history. No palliation can excuse it. No arm-chair theory of gradual evolution and ultimate purpose can wipe it out. If such theory proves anything it tells in the other direction, as establishing the incurable sinfulness of humanity and the martyrdom of man. One cannot dwell upon its poignant details. The slaves, packed in narrow stifling holds, chained and stapled to the floor, groaning with suffocation and nausea; the dead thrown overboard each morning. Death, it is said, released one in eight, on the voyage; a third as many passed away on landing, too near death to be fit to sell.

It is hard to believe that public feeling was so slow, that it took a hundred years to rouse even the first gusts of public indignation. But private greed, the thing called "business interest,"—almost as cruel as medieval bigotry,—covered up the sin. And even a hundred years later the history of the Congo and the Putumayo was to show that private greed is not done with us yet.

In any case, let it be repeated, the slave trade began in rougher days than ours as regards this matter of human indifference to physical suffering. In the seventeenth century barbarous cruelties were still everywhere practiced upon criminals and heretics. Burning and torturing were still judicially used. Nor were such things alone the perquisite of the Inquisition and the Church of Rome. "In Scotland," says the historian Lecky, "during nearly the whole period that the Stuarts were on the throne of England, a persecution rivaling in atrocity almost any on record was directed by the English government, at the instigation of the Scotch bishops and with the approbation of the English church. The Presbyterians were hunted like criminals over the mountains. Their ears were torn from the roots. They were branded with hot irons. Their fingers were

23

wrenched asunder by the thumbkins. The bones of their legs were shattered by the "boots." Women were scourged publicly through the streets. Multitudes were transported to Barbados, infuriated soldiers were let loose upon them and encouraged to exercise all their ingenuity in torturing them."

The brutality of the criminal law was as great, or nearly as great, as the brutality of the law of religion. Even in the eighteenth century people, contrary to what is generally supposed, were still burned to death by law in England.

Our history has smothered up these things. Time's ivy has grown over them, and on them falls the evening light of retrospect. The ever-living legend of the "good old times" spreads a kindly mantle over the horrors of the past. But the horrors were there just the same. So it comes that we single out the slave trade, ignorant of the setting in which it stood, the foul dungeon, the flaming stake, and the unspeakable torture room.

In such an age who could spare a tear for the dumb suffering of the transported African.

When the opposition to the slave trade at last arose, it came as a part of that inner light which presently illuminated England and mankind. It came as a part of the sentiment for humanity, which began in the eighteenth century, to replace the theological rigor of the days before. As theological controversy faded, it gave place to a new pity for mankind. As the Kingdom of Heaven retreated into the background it gave place to the hope of a kingdom on earth. The idea of salvation for eternity was replaced by that of salvation here and now.

This new current was a mingling of many streams. There was the new humanity of the Quaker, disclaiming persecution and turning the other cheek to war. The Quakers led in emancipating slaves, in deprecating cruelty, in casting out those who followed the trade (1761). There was added the new humanity of literature, the idealism of Pope and Thomson and Cowper, contrasting with the wholesale damnation of Milton.

All such writers decried and denounced the slave trade. Many of them, ignorant of the realities of savage life, carried their ideas to excess in the myth of the "noble savage." Thus Pope from his garden at Twickenham sang of the "poor Indian whose untutored mind, sees God in clouds and hears Him in the wind." In reality the "untutored savage" in America needed no tutoring in cruelty or cannibalism.

But even the myth of the noble savage and of the unsullied state of nature as taught by Rousseau, though false in fact, helped on the cause of humanity. To this was added the matter-of-fact reasoning of Adam Smith and the snorting indignation of Doctor Johnson.

The law followed its usual office of certifying a fact and locking a door already shut. Such was the famous judgment of Lord Mansfield in 1772 declaring slavery non-existent in England.

In time things reach even Parliament. A Mr. David Hartney, in 1776, moved that the slave-trade was contrary to the laws of God and the rights of man. The members failed to see it, but the thing was started. Then began a war of pamphlets and speeches. A certain Thomas Clarkson, competing, in Latin, for a Cambridge prize on the subject of the slave-trade, wrote so well that he convinced himself and devoted his life to the cause. He found associates in such men as Granville Sharp, William Wilberforce, and Zachary Macaulay. Business interest, having no conscience, began to shift sides. Planters in Virginia could raise and sell slaves at a bigger profit without the foreign slave-trade.

Then finally, the great tidal wave of the revolutionary era carried all before it and swept away in a flood a whole litter of dead laws, dead religions and dead iniquities, to give place to new ones.

In spite of the persistent opposition of the House of Lords, a British act of 1807 ended the British trade in slaves. French colonial slavery and the French slave trade, already denounced by Condorcet, Brissot, Lafayette and the other apostles of liberty and equality in 1789, was overwhelmed in the San Domingo rising and vanished. In the United States the slave-trade, already denounced in the first draft of the Declaration of Independence as an atrocious crime of George III, was prohibited by Act of Congress in 1807. The other nations (Sweden 1813, the Dutch 1814) followed suit. Even the Congress of Vienna condemned the trade in principle.

From the Europe and America that joined in the great peace of 1815, the slave-trade was gone forever.

All this, however, was not a matter of slavery, nor of the buying and selling of slaves, but only of the foreign trade in slaves with its attendant cruelty and horror. Of those who opposed the trade only a minority would have denounced slavery itself.

Even after Lord Mansfield's judgment terminated slavery in the British Isles, slavery in the British dependencies went quietly on. There were slaves in all of the thirteen colonies that were soon to become the United States. At the moment of independence some 600,000 persons in a total colonial population of about three and a half million were held in bondage. Georgia, the youngest of the colonies, originally founded (1732) as a refuge for the meek and the oppressed, began its career as already said with neither rum nor slaves. But it found that even the meek, in those days, needed both. There were slaves, and always had been, in the British West Indies. There were slaves in the royal province of Nova Scotia. They helped, we are told, to build the settlement of Halifax. There were slaves in Canada when it was taken over in 1763 and their status continued undisturbed, even when the Loyalists moved in. There was a public sale of slaves in Montreal as late as 1797.

To the people of the later eighteenth century—to most people—the status of the slave still seemed more or less natural. Slave catching, the raiding of African villages, the wholesale slaughterings and burnings of the slave raiders, the hideous voyage across the equatorial ocean,—these things began to wear a different aspect. But not slavery. After all, the lot of a slave on a decent plantation could hardly be said to be worse in point of toil than the lot of a French peasant or an English laborer: no worse,—except *in idea*.

And hardly any slaves and very few masters had any ideas. The few who had, deplored the thing but saw nothing to be done about it. Indeed presently, as the factory system arose, the lot of the English industrial workers was harder than that of many of the plantation slaves. At least, there was no "cry of the children" from the cornfields.

But the main thing was that before the great rise of the cotton trade, slavery was scarcely worth while. It was dying out. It came to an end, practically of itself, in British North America and in the Northern States. Free labor paid better. When the Massachusetts courts decided that slavery was incompatible with the Declaration of Independence and with the Constitution of 1780, this did not operate a social revolution. The emancipation laws which followed in all the states north of Mason and Dixon's line occasioned no social upheaval.

But we are not to suppose that the new freedom of American independence brought about this emancipation. The statement of the Declaration of 1776 that "all men are created equal" was not intended to apply to negroes. It referred to *men*. A leading American historian tells us that "resistless logic of one burning sentence . . . wrought the downfall of slave institutions in the United States." This is only true if we cut the sentence loose from the meaning given to it by those who set their names to it.

Yet slavery was a moribund institution.

Even in the South, the institution of slavery, in George Washington's time, seemed to show signs of passing away. Not that it raised any social scandal.

But in the main it was scarcely worth while. In most cases it was probably not cruel. It was at least free from the brutal grasp of machinery, speeding up the working power of man beyond man's own endurance. It was machinery in Europe that presently reacted on slavery in America. Longfellow's slave, who lay dead beside the ungathered rice and felt no more the driver's whip, had been beaten to death, partly, by Lancashire. The train of slaves which cumbered a great household—George Washington had, in all, a hundred and eighty-eight indoors and out—must have been to a great extent idle chatterers, dear at the price. Slaves in America had to be supported in old age and in illness,—in Lancashire they could be turned out to die. Even in the field work out of doors, under decent or even half decent masters, the lot of the blacks—apart always from the *idea* of it—was not so bad. There was not as yet the hideous slave market of later days; the sales "down the river"; the transport in chains and fetters, the sight of which "put the iron" into the soul of young Abraham Lincoln; the moaning fugitives recaptured, all wounds and dust, that pierced John Hay to the heart; or the "chained slaves, the saddest faces I have ever seen" that inspired in the little boy who was to be Mark Twain a sullen anger against the world that never left him.

But all *that* represents the nineteenth century, when slavery had changed from a social institution to a social disease that must be extirpated with the knife.

The colonial slavery of Washington's day gave at least a great appearance of wealth and social distinction. Washington's domestic herd of a hundred and eighty-eight slaves was scarcely in the front rank. Charles Carroll of Carrollton, one of the signers of the Declaration of Independence and the Rockefeller of his day, had twice as many: and various big planters of the Mississippi region twice that again. Slave-holding indeed seemed like wealth. Slavery permitted the efflorescence of the "gentleman," the man who does not work—the ideal of the Greeks and the lost hope of today.

But it seems doubtful whether the great troops of slaves, were worth while in the economic sense. Free labor in North America, with the stimulus of liberty, the incentive of opportunity, and the magic of property, worked with an eagerness and efficiency never known to the serfs and laborers of Europe. Beside it the fettered negro was nowhere. All observers, from the days of Washington till the Civil War, noted the difference. Frederick Olmsted, writing in the closing days of slavery, said that the slaves "seemed to go through the motions of labor without putting strength into them." He claimed that a New Jersey farmer did as much work as four of them. Another visitor of the period, watching the slave at work with the hoe, said that their motion "would have given a quick working Yankee convulsions."

Indeed during the period just preceding and just following the American Revolution there was spreading a wide feeling that slavery was scarcely worth the while. It must not be supposed that this feeling was inspired by the new emancipation of independence. As already said the assertion that all men are created

equal was not meant for the negroes. Jefferson's orig
inal draft contained an indictment of George III
for having violated "the most sacred rights of life
and liberty of a distant people, who never offended
him, captivating them into slavery in another hemi-
sphere or to incur miserable death in their transpor-
tation thither." This remains as one of the supreme
hypocrisies of history. Even at that, Jefferson struck
out the clause out of deference to South Carolina
and Georgia which still wanted the trade and because his "northern brethren" felt a "little tender"
about the subject.

But many people, Jefferson among them, doubted
whether slavery was right and wondered what would
ultimately come of it. "I tremble for my country,"
he wrote in his *Notes on Virginia* (1781), "when I
reflect that God is just, that his justice cannot sleep
forever." Washington, writing in 1786, the year before the Constitution riveted slavery on the nation
for three generations, expressed the wish that some
way might be found "by which slavery may be abolished by slow, sure, and imperceptible degrees."
Gadsden of South Carolina called negro slavery a
crime. Henry Laurens, whose slaves were worth
£20,000, wrote to his son, "You know, my dear son,
I abhor slavery." He proposed to set free as many
as he dared, balancing his duty to his family and to
the community against his sense of righteousness,
and calling on Providence to help him in his per-
plexity. The patriotic Macon of North Carolina
said, "There is not a gentleman in North Carolina
who does not wish there were no blacks in the country."

In the North the case against slavery and its obvious economic futility was strong enough to terminate the institution. The Massachusetts courts read it out of the state by interpretation, but John Adams said that "the real cause was the multiplication of laboring white people." Pennsylvania adopted a gradual emancipation act in 1780, Connecticut and Rhode Island in 1784, New York in 1799, New Jersey in 1804. In Delaware and Maryland abolition failed, but narrowly. Thus the North and South fell apart, but the line of division for the time had but little meaning and indicated no bitterness. That waited for the recrudescence of slavery half a century later.

If slavery could have passed away in Washington's time it would have left no bitter memories. But it was not to be. On this world that seemed to be opening out into liberty, equality, and fraternity with the dreams of Rousseau, the enthusiasms of Brissot and Lafayette, the peace of Pitt and the pounds, shillings and pence of Adam Smith, broke the full fury of revolution and war. The question of liberty and slavery was overwhelmed for nearly a generation in what was called for a hundred years The Great War. When the storm passed the scene was all changed.

II

THE IRREPRESSIBLE CONFLICT

WITH the peace of 1815, Europe and America woke to a new industrial world. It is always thus. Forces which had been gathering before The Great War, ideas and policies that had been slumbering during the conflict, now broke over the surface of a liberated world.

We always speak of the industrial revolution as a phenomenon of the eighteenth century. This is true of its origins and its earlier stages. But the full reality of the changes it was to bring belong to the era after the Napoleonic war, the era of the great peace and the age of industry. Machinery and steam power were rapidly to transform the world. Capital took on an organization hitherto unknown. Industrial society was shaken into a new mobility. Migration moved in a flood. The exodus to America began.

It is true that the treaty of Ghent and the battle of Waterloo were followed by a severe "slump," as had been, contrary to all expectations, the short-lived peace of Amiens in 1802. We are beginning now to understand, dimly, the economics of war, its initial economic prosperity, its marvelous and sustained impetus, its exhaustion, the collapse that follows its close, and the upward rush of prosperity that presently ensues. These phases the world witnessed a hundred years ago and will see again.

For America the consequences were colossal. Immigration moved in a flood. In Washington's day we may estimate that about two or three thousand newcomers landed annually in America. When the tabulated returns begin (1820) they show 8,385 arrivals. In the year 1830 there came 20,000, and thirty years later the annual average stood at a quarter of a million. Famine and revolution drove out the distressed of Europe, while the hope of liberty attracted the brave.

This wave of migration profoundly affected the Northern States. It obliterated any lingering possibility of slavery. It reduced the negroes to an insignificant minority. And it stimulated further the great movement over the mountains to the Ohio Valley, the new land of promise. Settlement had begun immediately after independence. The States had wisely given the national congress the whole domain from the Ohio to the Mississippi: congress had thrown it open to settlement and, in accordance with the ideas of the day, kept slavery out of it.

The great epic of the moving frontier had begun. In the year when Napoleon first sat looking out over the waste of the South Atlantic, the little Abraham Lincoln, clinging to his mother's hand, walked in the silent forest of Indiana, looking for a home. One age ended as the other began. The moving figures shifted on the screen.

In the Southern States a great change was going

on, but of an opposite character. What happened there was destined to root slavery to the soil and to multiply the slaves. The industrial inventions in England in the eighteenth century had replaced domestic spinning and weaving by machine industry. Cartwright's invention of the power loom (1785) had supplied the driving force. The stress was now on obtaining material. For in invention each process stimulates the others. No part must lag behind. Invention carries an increasing premium. It becomes conscious and deliberate. Mankind invents the idea of invention. Thus Edmund Cartwright, who was a clergyman and knew nothing of power and nothing of looms, sat down to invent a power loom. And thus did a young man called Eli Whitney set himself to invent a cotton gin, and therewith affected the destiny of the world.

The new textile industry in England wanted fibrous material. There was not enough wool, not enough flax, not enough of anything. Cotton was known in America but little grown and little used. It had been brought from the Orient to the Guiana coast of South America. It was tried out here and there in the Southern colonies. But the varieties used were short in the fiber, and the seeds clung to the lint, defying the slow labor of the fingers that plucked it out. After the peace of 1783 a few bags of United States cotton found their way to Liverpool.

But the opportunity offered by the straining industry was colossal. Once get a plant with long fibers, and find a way to get the seeds out of it,— and the consequences would be incalculable.

35

So it was done. Experiments began with new seeds from the Bahamas and new methods of cultivation. Many planters, like the famous General Moultrie, failed utterly. But success came. Before the end of the century they were raising 200 pounds of cotton to the acre. Each negro produced—in money, over his keep—$300 to $500 a year. Planters grew rich overnight.

Whereupon Eli Whitney, a graduate of Yale, invented the cotton gin (1793) because it had to be invented. Here again was conscious invention, and simple enough at that,—wire teeth on a sort of buzz-saw scraping into the cotton to tear the lint from the seeds and scraping itself clean against another saw.

Within a generation the raising of cotton overtook and surpassed all the other agricultural industries of the South put together. In the closing years of the slavery régime the census of 1850 showed some 75,000 cotton plantations as against 15,000 in tobacco. Of the slaves of the period almost three-quarters raised cotton as against only 14 per cent in tobacco and 6 per cent in sugar. Here began the economic union of Lancashire and the South with Cotton as King. Nothing hampered it but the deadweight of the northern connection crippling southern commerce with the ligaments of a mechanics tariff. So at least the Southerners saw it.

When secession came, it had with it an economic motive as powerful as political hatred. Secession, to the people of Charleston, meant a brief conflict in arms, or none at all, and then a wave of opulent commerce that would revive in the southern sea-ports the departed glory of Venice.

With cotton came sugar. The Louisiana Purchase of 1803 opened up for the United States the raising of cane sugar in the Mississippi delta. There was a rush for sugar and slaves, the ocean trade in Africans being still open. The sugar plantations spread rapidly up the river. There were 308 of these estates soon after the peace of 1815, and by the year 1830 there were 691 with 36,000 working slaves and an output worth fifty million dollars.

The growth of the two great staples, cotton and sugar, restored prosperity to the other agricultural crops. Tobacco, rice and hemp were carried forward on the flood tide. With the closing of the Atlantic trade and the expansion of industry the market for slaves rose to pleasing proportions. Befor the cotton gin, a first-class slave,—the kind listed for sale as a "prime field hand,"—was worth not more than $300: he fetched $800 in 1808 and $1,100 in the market boom of the years that followed. Virginia, not being a sugar or cotton State, went into the business of raising slaves for sale. It was estimated that from 50,000 to 100,000 were sold or taken out of the State in a year. A Richmond estimate in the banner year 1836 put the export at 120,000.

From now on there was no talk of abolition south of the Mason and Dixon's line. Yet it was at this very time that slavery was assuming its most cruel features, was passing from the patriarchal to the commercial, and was breaking asunder the united commonwealth.

37

The outward and visible signs of the new disunion were not long wanting. As the Union expanded over the mountains and up the valley of the Mississippi, the question naturally arose, what about slavery? Its exclusion in 1787 from the Ohio Valley went without opposition. New states, it is true, had come into the Union balanced between slave and free; Vermont (1791) paired with Kentucky and so on. But there was nothing vital about the balance. But now times had changed. When the settlers went into Missouri and wanted to make of it a slave state facing, across the Mississippi, the free soil of Illinois, the nation burst suddenly into angry dissension. All the world has read of how the aged Jefferson said that the Missouri controversy had startled him like the sound of an alarm bell in the night. Foresight never carried further. Missouri was the beginning. For the moment, the controversy was settled on the fallacious principle of "this time but never again"—no more slavery, said Congress, north of the southern boundary of the State. Such a principle, as always, carried its own undoing. With the "Missouri Compromise" began the forty years of conflict that ended in secession.

For the time, political parties shunned the issue. The Democrats, once the Republican Democrats of the closing eighteenth century, were as old as the Union: they carried the slavery tradition as a part of it. The new party, that formed as the Whigs, aimed at progress, national improvements, canals, railroads and economic power. They could not disregard the South. In between the two were raised dissentient voices louder and fiercer as slavery hardened into the commercial exploitation of a sunken race and the internal traffic in slaves recalled in some measure the horrors of the ocean slave trade. These were the "abolitionists," calling presently for martyrdom and defying the Constitution. They were repudiated on every side. Such honest men as Abraham Lincoln scoffed at them.

To Missouri succeeded the Texas annexation (1845) and the Mexican War and conquests with a vast new territory opened for slaves states. Southern enthusiasts dreamed of Cuba, of West Indian annexation—a very empire of slavery—as out of touch with the nineteenth century as the bygone empire of the Pharaohs. The rest of the world meantime was shaking off the contamination of slavery. England bought out its colonial slaves in 1833, and rustled with Victorian righteousness. France followed in 1848. Portugal after that. Only the Dutch retained slavery in their vast East Indian possessions till American emancipation. In Western Europe the semi-slavery called serfdom had been smashed to pieces in France and southern Germany by the French Revolution. Prussia ended it in 1807. After the great peace the remnants of it were cleaned out of Austria and the union states. Europe west of Russia was free after 1848,—if only free to starve. In America even the Federated States of Mexico, of which Texas was then one,—abolished slavery in 1824 and had gradual extinction written into the Constitution. Republican South and Central America had finished with slavery (Buenos Aires 1813, Colombia 1821, etc.) and even with the color line. The United States in the middle nineteenth century found itself lined up with monarchial Brazil, with Spanish Cuba, with the Dutch East Indies and with the slave continent of native and Arab Africa. It seems strange that any one could have believed in the expansion and duration of the slave empire of the South. Yet the people of the South did, and the people of the North in a limited and grudging way accepted it.

One turns to the contemporary record of the times to get some idea of what slavery seemed like in the days of its last conflict, to those who saw it and to those who lived among it. Only thus can we measure the forces that cast up Abraham Lincoln to the surface and made him a prime instrument of human destiny. Take a few of the typical judgments on American slavery. One turns to the outsiders first. Here to America in 1842 came the youthful Charles Dickens whose phenomenal success with the *Pickwick Papers* (1836) and the books that followed, had lifted him to a public notoriety and public affection never known before in the world of letters. Brilliant, ardent and captivating, he landed in Boston in January 1842 to meet a national reception only equaled by that of the Marquis de Lafayette, eighteen years before. He left America five months later sickened and disillusioned and longing for home. The disinterested radical longed for monarchy. Dickens never understood America. In the epic of the conquest of the frontier (he went as far as the Mississippi), he saw only the squalor of crowded steamers, the loneliness of log cabin settlements, the braggart voices, the lack of manners and the universal flood of tobacco spit.

The genius that could turn to kindly amusement the filth of a London slum and could transform the brutality of a Squeers and the rascality of an Alfred Jingle,—utterly failed in America. Most of all he was repelled by slavery, not the fact of it, for he practically never saw it, but by the thought of it. The very idea of human bondage struck into his soul.

Charles Dickens, writes his latest biographer, "did not stop to ask, he did not care to know, whether the plantation slave was happier than the factory hand of Lancashire, whether the slave himself felt the degradation of his chain or only the weight of it. —Dickens wanted nothing of such talk. He felt, as Longfellow felt, or Channing, that the thing was utterly and hideously wrong in itself, and different from any form of want or suffering that might arise where at least the will is free. Like all the people of his day, he valued individual freedom, if only freedom to die of starvation. Many of us still share his view.

"His attitude towards slavery separated Dickens in thought and sympathy from the South. People who lived among slavery took it as they found it—a sort of way of living and working. There were good owners and bad, kind and cruel; but cruelty to any real extent was the exception, not the rule. A slave minded the whip as much and as little as did an Eton schoolboy. He measured it by the sting, not by the moral. People who owned slaves shuddered at the sight of an English factory—its close mephitic air, its clattering machinery, the pale, wan faces working at the looms in the gaslight, the hideous

41

toll of the twelve and fourteen hours of work extracted from little children; the long lines of starving people clamoring for bread in the England of the hungry 'forties and receiving as their answer the cold lead of the Waterloo musket. They contrasted this with the bright picture of the cornfield, bathed in wind and sun, the negroes singing at their work, and the little pickaninnies clinging to the red gowns of their mothers. On such people of the South in the days of the 'forties descended a fury of anger when a pert Mrs. Trollope, or a prim old maid Harriet Martineau, or a young Mr. Dickens, fresh from the miseries of the English factory and the London slum, should hold up their hands in pious horror over the cheerful darkey of the sunny South. They were no doubt wrong. To many of us, one single family broken up and sold down the river outbalances the whole of Lancashire."

But we must remember that Dickens represents the type of person who denounced slavery without seeing it, whose abhorrence arose from the idea of it and not from experience of it. We may place beside it the judgment of other foreigners who saw slavery on the spot and whose standing and eminence entitled their views to respect: among these one thinks of Sir Charles Lyell, the great geologist; Harriet Martineau, the Victorian spinster of a hundred works; Captain Basil Hall and Captain Marryat, as British naval men not overgiven to sentiment; Chevalier, French economist and official, visiting America (1836) on a government mission. All these came to America before the closing decade of the 'fifties overwhelmed the slavery question in a maelstrom of prejudice and hatred. What did they think?

Sir Charles Lyell, the great geologist, visited America and traveled extensively in 1841 and in 1845. He was primarily interested in such things as the "retrogression" of Niagara Falls, the vegetation of the Dismal Swamp of Virginia and the alluvium of the Mississippi Delta. But he had an eye, also scientific and neutral, for manners and customs. Lyell noted the planters' style of living, "like that of English country gentlemen," the family pride of the planters; the cleanliness of the plantation hospitals for the sick slaves; the negro merriment at Christmas, "a kind of Saturnalia," and sums it up that he saw "little actual suffering" in the South.

But almost at the same time with Sir Charles, there traveled in America a Mr. Alexander Mackay, correspondent of the London *Morning Chronicle,* reporting on the Oregon dispute. He agrees with Lyell about the dignity and pride of the older plantations but fiercely denounces the change wrought by the cotton plantation. There slavery "appears in its true light, in its real character, in all its revolting atrocities. In the practical working of slavery in the cotton growing districts, humanity is the exception and brutality the rule."

Captain Basil Hall was a British naval officer of the Napoleonic war on active service from the peace of Amiens to Waterloo. After that he traveled the world over and wrote it up in about twelve volumes. He certainly should have known something. Of his travels in America in 1827 and 1828 he writes, "I have no wish, God knows, to defend slavery in the abstract but nothing gave me more satisfaction than the conclusion to which I was gradually brought that the planters of the Southern States, generally speaking, have a sincere desire to manage their estates with the least possible severity." Nor did he think the work as hard as that of the "hired man" of the North. "In Carolina," he writes, "all mankind appeared comparatively idle."

Hall's fellow naval officer, the famous Captain Marryat of the sea-stories, visiting America in 1837, takes slavery pretty much as he finds it with no great oratory. But he tells some appalling stories of exceptional cases of what slavery could mean.

Miss Harriet Martineau was a super-gifted English spinster, who embodied in herself the whole generation of Queen Victoria. She was as quick as a needle: she never stopped writing; and she had no more originality than a hen. Her mind, truly feminine, was just a reflection of the ideas of her time. But she wrote in all about a hundred books. In her account of her travels in the United States (*Society in America,* 1837) she paid full tribute to the charm and politeness of southern society, was fascinated by the languor and grace of Charleston, and its profuse hospitality. She admitted the care and kindliness of most southern masters and said that "nothing struck her more than the patience of the slave-owners with their slaves." But the institution itself she could not tolerate: and people told her ghastly stories, probably untrue, of slaves worked to death on purpose on the sugar plantations.

Miss Martineau had a lot to say also about the status and lot of the negro woman. There she "got it all wrong," confusing the ideas of a Victorian spinster with those of a rotund black woman only two generations out of equatorial Africa. Miss Harriet should have gone and lived for a while in the place where the negroes came from. After that she would have had no fear of the whites corrupting their morals. But most of all Harriet Martineau gave unpardonable offense to the South by openly espousing the cause of the abolitionists, whose treatment she described in the Westminster *Review* as the "martyr age of the United States."

The name of Michael Chevalier, a by-gone authority on gold and free trade, still echoes in the gloomy Pantheon of political economy. The French government sent him to America to study the canal and transport system, a visit chronicled in his *Society, Manners and Politics in the United States* (1839). His judgment of slavery is interesting,— that it is physically all right, but morally and socially impossible and doomed. He thought that even the Americans still wanted to get rid of it,—"a scourge to all the countries in which it exists: of this the people of the United States in the South as well as in the North are convinced." But he adds to this:

"It is just to observe that, in the United States, the slaves, though intellectually and morally degraded, are humanely treated in a physical point of view. They are less severely tasked, better fed, and better taken care of, than most of the peasants of Europe."

This from a man of high intelligence, trained in observation, and biased in the other direction, is notable testimony.

Chevalier, however, never saw the cotton states. But even in Richmond, slavery hit him hard.

"There is something in Richmond," he writes, "which offends me even more than its bottomless mudholes and shocks me more than the rudeness of the Western Virginians, whom I met here during the session of the legislature; it is slavery. Physically the negroes are well used in Virginia, partly from motives of humanity, and partly because they are so much livestock raised for exportation to Louisiana: morally they are treated as if they did not belong to the human race. Free or slave, the black is here denied all that can give him the dignity of man. The law forbids the instruction of the slave or the free men of color in the simplest rudiments of learning under the severest of penalties; the slave has no family; he has no civil rights; he holds no property. The white man knows that in secret the negro broods over hopes and schemes of vengeance and that the exploits and martyrdom of Gabriel, the leader of an old conspiracy, and of Turner, the hero of a more recent insurrection, are still related in the negro cabins."

On this last point Chevalier was undoubtedly in error. The negro hoped for nothing and brooded over nothing.

Let it be noted, for what it signified, that the negroes, all through the slavery conflict, never rose, never even budged. The slave insurrection was a mere dream, a nightmare. The slaves went on playing the banjo and drowsily moving the hoe. They planned nothing. They harbored no hatred. The age-long children of destiny, they took their lot as

46

they found it. They had no part in the fierce vindictive angers of the overfed white race, that passed in thunder over their heads. Even when the war came the slaves never rose and never thought of it. That large fact should never be forgotten in the record.

Set beside the foreign arguments, as typical of the lives and thoughts of millions of people in America, the words of one of the wisest men who ever lived with slavery and saw it go.

This is Mark Twain speaking of his mother,—

"My mother had been in daily touch with slavery for sixty years. Kind-hearted and compassionate as she was, I think she was not conscious that slavery was a bald, grotesque and unwarrantable usurpation. She had never heard it attacked in any pulpit, but had heard it defended and sanctified in a thousand. . . .

"As a rule our slaves were convinced and content. . . . It was the mild domestic slavery, not the brutal plantation article. . . . The 'nigger trader' was condemned by everybody, a sort of human devil who bought and conveyed poor helpless creatures to hell."

These all—the Dickenses and the Martineaus and the Basil Halls—were foreign travelers and observers. It is only fair to record that most foreigners, who stayed at home and never saw American slavery, accepted it easily enough. There was no international outcry against it. In England some people accepted it as other people's trouble, easily borne; some, like the cotton spinning Gladstones, from business interest, as a part of the greatness of Lancashire; others as biblical and patriarchal fitting in with the squire and parson at home; others like Thomas Carlyle for the pleasure of disagreement and from the egotism of indigestion.

On one count or another there were plenty of pro-slavery, or pro-American slavery people in England.

At home the people in the South overwhelmingly accepted it. They lived too close to it to think of theories. It was their way of life. But naturally, as discussion multiplied they rallied to its defense. Argument, itself, presently deepened their conviction.

People of station, clergymen and college teachers of the South set forth the articles of their faith. There was Dr. Thomas Cooper of Carolina College who showed, as political economy (1826), that a slave who got his board and his keep and decent treatment got more than he was worth,—a woolly argument which led nowhere. Professor Thomas Dew of William and Mary did better by laying stress on the happiness of the slave, the "naturalness" of his condition and the scriptural warrant for it. Dew's *Essay* (originally published in 1852) was followed by Harper and Hammond and other exponents and became the basis of the defense of the institution by all the honest pro-slavery men of the South, who wrote it fearlessly and defiantly into their constitution of 1861.

But Southern argument could no longer remain calm and academic when it was goaded to frenzy by the assaults of the rising abolitionists.

As the century wore on and the slave question

ate into the national life, the abolition propaganda
had changed from calm philosophy to fiery denunciation, from argument to martyrdom, from words
to threats and blood. Abolitionists forgot the means
in the end. They accused the Southerners of cruelty,
lust and crime. They called on America to spurn
the constitution as "a covenant with death and an
agreement with hell." Such men as the Reverend
Stephen Foster denounced the Southern churches,
—"every communicant worse than a pickpocket and
an assassin." The Reverend George Brown denounced the (imaginary) slave market, foul, drunken
and obscene. In Boston Theodore Parker and Wendell Phillips urged the breaking of the law. "Ac-
cursed be the American Union," rang out the
Liberty Bell of 1845. William Lloyd Garrison, the
patron saint of abolition, matched against the constitution the texts of Christ's new testament and
declared that the covenant of death must be an-
nulled.

Others, the open incendiaries, went further still.
John Hill, an escaped slave, called aloud for "blood,
death and liberty." Frederick Douglass, a negro,
urged the slaves to rise in arms. This, ever since
Nat Turner of Virginia, a negro preacher, a mut-
tering mystic, had gone amuck (1831) with a clut-
tering of crazy followers, and butchered women and
children,—this had been the slumbering dread of
the South. To preach this was death.

The approaching convulsion of society was being
made, said the Southerners, not by the slaves but
by the abolitionists. Yet the abolitionists had begun
as a people of the inner light. Were they wrong?

Each must judge them for himself. But at least it can be noted that what they demanded was abolition, immediate and without compensation, and they claimed that slavery was contrary to the mind of God. This is exactly what Lincoln did in his proclamation of 1863, and exactly what he said in his second inaugural address.

Meantime, as the current moved faster towards the abyss, the politicians, after their manner, did nothing, or nothing real and final. The Democrats wouldn't and the Whigs couldn't. Both wanted votes and office. Neither could live except astride of slavery and freedom. They must ride two horses or fall. In 1850, as every reader knows, they patched up a "Great Compromise" that settled nothing; slavery in the South and at the capital, and perhaps in the Southwest, and a fugitive slave law,—and round it all a hedge of doubt and uncertainty. The compromise settled nothing. It carried down with it the reputation of Clay and Webster. But beyond that it merely shifted the scenes for the closing act of the ten years' drama that was to end in secession.

III

LINCOLN IN ILLINOIS

NOW there was living all this time in Illinois a tall, ungainly man whose name was Abraham Lincoln. And this was an inspired man, an instrument of human destiny. But the vision that was to make him so had not yet come.

Lincoln stood six feet four in his stockinged feet. He had a frame of great strength, proportionated after that of an ape, with hands swinging almost at his knees. He was, literally, one of the strongest men in all the world.

Round the name of Abraham Lincoln there has gathered one of the great myths of history. He is credited with capacities which he never had and with a foresight that he never showed. Nearly everything about his career is seen in a false light and glorified beyond recognition. The ignorance and ineptitude in which he assumed the presidency of the United States are now lost in the accumulation of panegyric and reverence. To say anything derogatory to his memory seems like the desecration of a grave.

But in reality the truth about Abraham Lincoln is better than the myth.

In his own day Lincoln was, till the very end, the

object of hatred and mockery from millions who were his opponents: of contempt and ridicule, for years, from millions whom fate made his adherents: of doubt and distrust, for at least half his time in office, from many of those who worked beside him. But underneath this and through this, there grew the sublime faith of millions, the roaring plaudits of marching armies, whose voices went up in chorus to "Father Abraham," the lamp of hope lit in the humble home, the pardons without hatred, the rebukes without anger, the wide humanity which in the end brought humanity to his feet,—and, at the last, martyrdom in the moment of achievement.

In the face of all this and the universal reverence that has grown out of it, it sounds like the babbling of a fool or the blasphemy of an idiot to cast doubt on Lincoln's political career, of his fitness for the presidency or his policy towards secession. Who dares suggest that when he assumed the office he was lost, ignorant and incompetent, without a policy, without a plan, a man adrift upon a sea of trouble. Yet that is true. Not till he liberated the slaves in America did Lincoln liberate his own soul. Till then what is there to admire? Excepting always the inspiration of his soul, which in the end was to achieve his greatness.

For the truth about Lincoln is better than the myth about his prescience and capacity, his political foresight and diplomatic insight. He had little of these things and very little available for effective use in 1861. But the truth is that Lincoln was one of the elect of mankind. Underneath and unknown, he had an inspired soul. He was instinct with a love and pity for all mankind comparable to that which has carried the name of Jesus Christ down twenty centuries. He could not hate even a slaveholder.

All of this was underneath, distant, unconscious,

WHAT WILL HE DO WITH THEM?
(*From* Vanity Fair, *October, 1862*)

not yet realized. Yet there was a foreboding of it in the strange melancholy of Lincoln's face, the deep lost meaning of his eye. It was this inner look that changed his whole aspect. For each of us there comes at times a sentience of the personality of others. It is the universal, the immortal part of us,—reaching across. In this hangs the art of mystic healing, the appeal of oratory and much else.

53

Such was the "impression" conveyed by Abraham Lincoln.

Without this inner light Lincoln would have been a comic figure. At times he almost was. When they presently inaugurated him as the president of the United States, his clumsy gestures, his awkward clothes, his dilemma over his big Bible and his huge walking stick and his new hat, should have made him—almost did make him—ridiculous. There were those living not long ago who could remember seeing him riding beside his soldiers,—a grotesque figure in a stovepipe hat and an ill-fitting suit, his trailing legs too long for the horse,—a very Don Quixote of comicality,—but converted from ridicule to glory.

This impression that Lincoln gave, this saddened aspect, made people instinctively speak of him as old. "Honest Old Abe" was the name he carried in Springfield long before the world had heard of him. Yet he was not very old and not so desperately honest.

For honesty was not entirely his trade, at least not till later in life. As a lawyer Lincoln was absolutely and peculiarly honest, as honest as any one can be in that amiable profession which keeps its own moral department as the "ethics of advocacy." But Lincoln was also a "politician." In that capacity he was just like the rest. The politician learns to traffic in committees and platforms, caucuses and gerrymanders: office means too much to him: truth too little. The politician learns to confuse a platform with a principle, a unanimous vote with general agreement and a majority vote with a moral sanction. This was especially so in peace, in the formative era of democracy groping its way into the art of government. This was the cause of shipwreck of the Websters and the Clays.

Deep under the litter and rubble of the political surface lies, no doubt, the bed-rock of character and opinion. In time of peace, it is concealed. War lays it bare.

Thus naturally in a backwoods career like that of Lincoln "politics" played too large a place. He knew the tricks of the trade and he used them. Left to himself he would have been an abolitionist,— minus the hatred and invective. But backwoods politics dimmed the inner light. Lincoln thought of slavery in terms of parties and platforms. It was only when he was lifted up so high that he stood alone and isolated, with nothing between him and the infinite, that he found another vision.

Abraham Lincoln was born on February 12, 1809. He came of the plainest sort of log-cabin people of the American frontier. His father moved from one shanty in the wilderness to another. His was the instinct of the frontiersman, building a cabin in the bush and then, as settlers came and the bush changed to farm and road and village, moving on again.

Such people as Thomas Lincoln lived in log huts, with holes for windows, with wooden slabs for chairs and tables, and with a few pots and pans brought with them from the "settlements." Their sole treasured possessions, priceless beyond words, were their rifle and powder horn, and their ax. The men dressed in deerskins, foul and redolent in the damp, wore moccasins in place of shoes,—the dress of savages. Their food was game, plentiful but ill-cooked, without sauce or spice, corn from the patches among the trees. Sugar they had none, except as squeezed from wild honey. Their drink was water, and whisky crudely made, untaxed and deadly in its potency. All about them was the dripping malarial forest, the fierce dry heat of midsummer and the intermittent cold of winter, at times intense.

Theirs was not so much out-of-doors life as out-of-doors exposure. The men in spite of their iron frames and strong limbs were old at forty. Compare these types:—the Illinois pioneer of the backwoods, his tawny face lined and furrowed and ageless at forty years, and the English gardener of the same period on whose countenance the wind and the rain and the petals of the rose had fallen so gently as to leave it pink and white at seventy, his eyes a china-blue vacuity and his brain still undisturbed. Yet these were cousins. By a slight shift of circumstance either might have been the other.

Of intellectual life the settlers had and needed little or none. A few tattered books were trailed from cabin to cabin. Odd people taught the children their letters in a deserted shed, miscalled a school. Itinerant preachers moved through the bush, conducting domestic prayer in return for meals and a bed, and at times providing the settlers with the emotional hysteria of a "camp meeting."

But no one can understand the circumstances of Lincoln's life without realizing that this environment of the frontier was a moving, changing phenomenon. Within a little time it was, in any locality, all completely changed. First there was the unbroken forest, charted only by rivers,—silent, untenanted. The savages, except in little clusters here and there, were but few,—random hunters along the forest trails. Then came the earliest pioneers, floating down from the upper rivers on rafts or scows to find new homes. Thus floated (in 1816) Thomas Lincoln, with his pots and pans and kettles and tools and 400 gallons of whisky as the movable wealth of forest commerce. He was looking for a likely place—one lonely enough for a frontiersman.

After such first migrations came further settlers in a stream that spread and widened through the forest and out into the park land and the prairie. The forest fell before the ax. Great piles of timber, priceless today, went up in smoke. The rude cabins were replaced by frame houses. The clearings joined together to make fields. Roads struck through the woods. Crossroads, blacksmith shops, and river sawmills expanded into villages with courts, and schools and churches. The steamboat came, sending aloft the sparks of its wood fires, waking the wilderness by day and lighting it by night. And with the steamboat there poured in a flood of settlers, a tide of immigrants, good and bad, settlers and adventurers, pioneers on foot, with women and little children peeping from the wagon hoods.

It is a great epic in the history of America,—the invasion of the Mississippi valley and its transformation in one generation at the hands of man.

So it came that within the childhood and earlier life of Abraham Lincoln and his contemporaries the world about them was transformed. The Spring Creek in the wilderness of Illinois became the frontier village of Springfield, then a trim town, a rising city, a railroad center and the capital of the State. All this places behind the events of the time not a background but a moving picture. There was nothing of this in the Old World. But we cannot understand America and things American without it. The London to which the little Charles Dickens traveled in a coach from Chatham was, with no vital difference, the same town in which he lived and died. The Indiana to which was led through the forest the little Lincoln, Dickens's contemporary, was a quite different place from the Indiana that sent its numbered regiments to Lincoln's service in the Civil War.

Thomas Lincoln found a likely place on a forest stream,—Little Pigeon Creek in Indiana and went back and fetched his wife and his two children, Abraham and Sarah. He made a sort of shelter out of poles, three sides closed to the weather and one open. There the family lived for a year, while the father cut logs for a cabin and cleared a patch for corn.

For fourteen years the Lincolns lived in this cabin. It had for two years no doors, no windows. Little Abraham slept on a bed of leaves on the poles that made a "loft." A few other settlers straggled to Pigeon Creek, among them Lincoln's relatives, the Sparrows. In the second year came malaria and malignant fever, bred in the dripping woods. Among those who died were the Sparrows, husband and wife, and Lincoln's mother (Oct. 5, 1818). Thomas Lincoln made three coffins "out of green lumber cut with a whipsaw" and buried the bodies in the clearing. It was little Lincoln's first vision of death.

There was no burial ceremony till months later an itinerant preacher read the funeral service over the snow that covered the grave.

In such a place a man could not live alone. A year later Thomas Lincoln made a journey back to Kentucky and brought home a new wife. This Sarah Lincoln was a kind, energetic woman. She brought with her quite a stock of household goods. She made clothes for the little boy and his sister, and beds. She was a real mother.

Abraham Lincoln passed his childhood in this log cabin. He had a little schooling, from itinerant teachers in odd houses and shelters. To his last "school" the boy walked, to it and back, nine miles a day. He had, in all, perhaps a year of teaching. He learned to "read and write and cipher."

Beyond that, all that he ever knew Lincoln taught himself. There were a few odd books in the settlement. Lincoln, by the firelight, pored over *Æsop's Fables, Robinson Crusoe,* the *Life of Washington* (the cherry-tree one of Mr. Weems) and some forgotten *History of the United States.* His mind was slow, but an innate passion for learning drove it on. He wrote down sentences and phrases and learned them by heart. To save paper, a rarity, he wrote on a wooden shovel and shaved off the sums and the compositions to make place for the next ones.

All this time the settlement grew. There were "raisings" of new houses, the building of a church, the opening of a court. And with the settlement grew young Abraham, taller and longer with every year, rising to that incredible physical strength and the great height that marked him out even among frontiersmen. At eighteen he stood to his full height of six feet four. His strength was colossal. His feats became legendary. He could lift and carry away 600 pounds. He could pick up a barrel of whisky in his hands and drink out of the taphole: the whisky, they said, he spat out afterward. Liquor and tobacco, even in that age of drinking and chewing, he never touched.

His life and work were those of the bush farm: the clearing of trees, the breaking of the ground with yoked oxen, the plow, the harrow and the "cradle," the care and watering of the stock. After the long day's work came the long summer evening loud with insect and cricket; the long winter night with the bright silence of the moonlit snow; the hard, fresh call of spring with the frogs trilling in the marsh.

It was the routine of life, still remembered by many of us in old age, before the city and its apparatus laid its hand across our continent and claimed it.

As the settlement expanded, Lincoln's life expanded with it. Near to his cabin home grew up the hamlet, the village, of Gentryville. Settlers moved in an unending procession down the rivers, heading west. Young Lincoln worked at a ferry crossing (Anderson's Creek); he saw the world come and go. Not far away the famous English apostle Robert Owen had founded peace on earth at New

Harmony on the Wabash. Lincoln saw Owen's queer disciples float past.

Once, at sixteen years of age, he went right down the Ohio and far down on the Mississippi as a hand on a flatboat. He saw bush settlements and wharves and steamboats, towns rising out of clap-board lumber and "niggers" skulking in the bush.

All this was the difference between America and Europe. In America the life of the individual and the life of society moved together into the unknown.

But the settlements were becoming too crowded for Lincoln's father. In the early spring of 1830 he moved on west, family and all. This time they passed over prairie like a park with cabins and farmsteads springing everywhere in the rich soil. Lincoln, a youthful giant, made the wagon, and hewed and hauled the logs for the new house. They settled in Coles County, Illinois, a district already loud with the hammer and the ax, with civilization closing in on it.

Again Lincoln went "down the river," this time all the way to New Orleans. Here he had his first vision of a city, and with it his first real view of slavery. It is true that Lincoln's eyes had opened upon slavery in his infancy in Kentucky. There were slaves even in the mean settlement where he was born. People who had one or two "niggers" as slaves were better than people like Thomas and Nancy Lincoln who had none. Slavery even there inserted the poison of social divergence among its masters. But in Indiana, in the bush clearing, there were no slaves and no use for them. Slaves cannot

61

live in a one-room cabin where the children sleep in a loft.

But "down the river" Lincoln saw for the first time what slavery meant. "At New Orleans," so wrote afterwards his kinsman, John Hanks, who went with him, they "saw negroes chained, maltreated, whipped and scourged. Lincoln saw it; his heart bled; he said nothing much, was silent, looked sad. I can say, knowing it, that it was on this trip that he formed his opinion of slavery. It run [*sic*] its iron in him there and then, May 1831. I have heard him say so, often."

In the sympathetic sense no doubt this is true. But not in the political. Lincoln's mind moved too slowly for that; his knowledge was too immature, his outlook too limited. He might sorrow for the slaves but he could tolerate the institution. As late as March 4, 1861, he would have kept every one of the five million slaves under what he called in 1865 the "bondsman's unrequited toil," rather than break the union of the States.

It is falsifying history to say that Lincoln was ever an active opponent of the institution of slavery, until his eyes opened upon his mission to destroy it. To "limit" slavery to a quarter of a continent, to prophesy its "ultimate extinction,"—there is nothing heroic in this. If the iron was in his soul, he carried it politically, for thirty years.

In short, it is not possible to straighten out Lincoln's views on the place of slavery in American life without taking account of the gradual opening of his mind; the gradual awakening of his soul.

But all that great change was as yet latent and far

away. For the time, as with each of us, his mind and thought and energy was set upon the little circuit of his own life.

It is beside the present purpose to follow in detail the stages of Lincoln's earlier career, in farm and bush, and country store and village politics. It is a record shared with uncounted thousands of the unknown. Apart from his great strength, his tolerant good nature and a queer "something" about him, Lincoln was much like the rest.

He did not long remain on his father's new place at Goose Neck Prairie in Coles County. He had no intention of being a farmer. Seeking a larger life Lincoln moved into New Salem, Illinois, a rising hamlet that as yet only meant a sawmill and a tavern and one or two frame shops. Lincoln started as a clerk in a store, tried storekeeping in partnership and storekeeping on his own account and failed at it all three ways.

But his great strength, his easy temperament and his odd mind soon made him a great favorite in the place. There was in particular a gang of toughs around the settlement, nicknamed the Clary Grove Boys, for whom Abraham Lincoln was at first a new victim and presently a leader and a hero. When the governor of Illinois called for volunteers to go out and repel the Indian intrusion of the northwest of the State (The Black Hawk War, 1832) Lincoln and his new friends trooped off together as volunteers. They elected him captain. In return he let them do as they liked. It is said that the officers of the United States army present with the expedition had their own opinion of Lincoln as an officer. At any rate he was not Napoleon. Later on in a well-known speech in Congress Lincoln gave a somewhat comical account of his war service, as a political way of hitting at the equally bloodless General Cass. But in reality, though he saw no fighting, he witnessed something of the meaning of war. Once he and his fellows found and buried a little cluster of the newly dead, their faces, in Lincoln's own words "painted all over" with the sunset.

Lincoln came back,—and went on failing. The truth is he had a mind too large for business, too honest for petty gain. Nor had he the stern determination and the fixed industry of a Carnegie or a Strathcona. Lincoln's industry is another legend and myth. In reality he was always a queer mixture of application and idleness. To certain things which appealed to his mind he applied himself with extraordinary zeal, reading day and night. He would read Greek History by candlelight in a hotel bedroom till two in the morning, his bedfellow (in those days gentlemen on circuit slept two in a bed) snoring beside him. He would coil himself in impossible attitudes, or possible only to him, doubled in a hoop, as he read, and lost to the world.

But in the main, Lincoln disliked work. There was in him much of the loafer of the country store: he could sit on a cracker barrel for hours, engaged in idle gossip or story-telling. It was a habit that never left him. The White House presently became his cracker barrel.

But from the first "politics" and the hope of office drew him on: not as a means of doing good to his fellowmen; that came later: of that, Lincoln had in the early Illinois days about as much and as little as the rest of us in America. "Politics" meant to Abraham Lincoln the opportunity of a man of parts to make his way easily in the world.

He was put up as a candidate for the legislature in 1832, just after the Indian expedition. He failed for office. But in 1834, still impecunious and unsuccessful and carrying along a cloud of debt, he was elected.

He borrowed two hundred dollars from a friend, bought a store suit, and in due course (1835) took his seat at Vandalia. Lincoln's first two years in the legislature were quite undistinguished: he introduced a few unimportant bills and led in the "logrolling" that moved the capital from Vandalia to Springfield. But at least Lincoln came out as poor as he went in: and at least he enhanced his reputation as a story-teller, a considerable asset in politics. "After a day of legislative session," says an enthusiastic biographer, "Lincoln enjoyed sitting in a hotel room with friendly souls, sitting with his knees up to his chin, drawling out stories, talking of how they were beating the Democrats, emphasizing a good point by drawing his knees again up to his chin, and letting both feet fall down to the floor with a slam."

But one episode of Lincoln's career in the legislature at Vandalia is worth more than a passing reference. The slavery dispute, as already seen, the Missouri Compromise, was beginning to echo through the nation. The cry of the abolitionists was already loud. Southern newspapers were calling for hanging them.   President Jackson was speaking out his mind.   He had suggested to Congress to pass "such a law as will prohibit under severe penalties the circulation in the Southern States incendiary publications intended to instigate the slaves to insurrection."   Already in South Carolina there was talk of seceding out of the Union.   And Jackson had answered *that* with the public declaration, "To say that any State may at pleasure secede from the Union is to say that the United States are not a nation."   To this Jackson added in a personal message to the government of South Carolina, "Tell them if one South Carolina finger be raised in defiance of this government that I shall come down there: and once I am there I will hang the first man I can lay my hands on, to the first tree I can reach."

If Lincoln had said that when his turn came, one wonders what would have happened.

In 1837 the Illinois legislature passed a resolution saying, "We highly disapprove of the formation of abolition societies.   The right of property in slaves is secured to the slaveholding States by the Federal constitution.   They cannot be deprived of that right without their consent."

Lincoln and one other member dissented.   In a protest written into the Journal they said: "The undersigned believe that the institution of slavery is founded on both injustice and bad policy but that the promulgation of abolition doctrines tends rather to increase than to abate its evils.

"They believe that the Congress of the United States has no power under the constitution to inter-

66

fere with the institution of slavery in the different States.

"They believe that the Congress of the United States has the power, under the constitution, to interfere with slavery in the district of Columbia, but that the power ought not to be exercised unless at the request of the people of the district."

This "protest" is exactly Lincoln, exactly his "protest" and the dilemma of his mind from 1837 till 1862. It shows what he believed to be wrong, and what he tried to think was right. Slavery was a wicked thing. But the Federal government must not try to alter it. It's a hard saying.

But as yet Lincoln was not concerned over the dilemma. Slavery was little in his thoughts as yet. He had other hopes and sorrows that seemed deeper.

For at this time, his first, his only real love had come into Lincoln's life. This was his courtship of Anne Rutledge, a settler's daughter of his own class and kind. His love for her had in it all the beauty and disinterestedness that goes with the morning of life. Anne was only eighteen. Together they sat and made plans that she should go to a college, a new "Female Academy" at Jacksonville: education seemed a wonderful thing: Lincoln, too, would go to a "college." He would arrange to get out of classes to sit in the legislature. Looking back on it the strange reversal of values touches on pathos,—to get a holiday from parliament to take first-year Latin.

Then came over the settlement a visitation of ague and malaria such as had swept away Lincoln's mother. And when it had passed, Anne Rutledge was gone. After her death Lincoln sat for hours, speechless, without answering. There came over him then and in the year that followed long spells of melancholy, such as the first realization of our human lot forces upon the young. It is youth's questioning of the meaning of life. Old age is glad to live on without question. Later both life and its question fade together.

Thus love touched Abraham Lincoln's life and passed. There was presently a slap dash affair with a temporary engagement with a certain lively and bouncing Miss Mary Owens,—the "friend Mary" of Lincoln's letters. But it came to nothing. Later there was a marriage that came to less. But love was over.

Lincoln went back again to more storekeeping, still a failure: learned surveying and found a job or two in it. For a time he was postmaster at New Salem, another cracker-barrel occupation. Then in a fortunate moment he began to borrow law books from a Springfield friend and to equip himself for the law.

In those days it was easy in Illinois to become a lawyer as it was to become a statesman or a captain. The study of books and acceptance by the local bar was enough. Moving to Springfield was the natural thing to do since the legislature had already gone there, and Lincoln, debts and all, was reëlected again and again and sat from 1835 till 1843. A contemporary and friend looking back from later life and speaking in affectionate praise said, "He was a born politician."

68

Abraham Lincoln came to Springfield to practice law as a partner with John T. Stuart, the man who had lent him the books. He remained as a lawyer in Springfield till he left it on a February morning in 1861 on the journey from which he never returned. His Springfield life lasted for nearly twenty-four years. Till near the end of it he was quite unknown to the outside world, though he sat once for two years in Congress.

The Springfield of that day (1837) was a place of 1500 people, with a fine farm country round it, rising fast,—banks, stores, taverns and church multiplying every year.

There was not much practice at first, a few odd fees that kept Lincoln existing somewhere between poverty and penury. But if not business at least there was lots of "politics." Lincoln was in the legislature and Stuart running for Congress against Stephen Douglas, later the "little giant." There were plenty of stump speeches, fights and excitement. Board only cost $1.50 a week. No one was rich. The world around was moving and expanding. There was an individual prominence, lost in later decades. Everybody was somebody. Life is easily magnified in new and rising places, in "boom" towns and mushroom "cities." Charles Dickens complained (in 1842) that every American seemed to think every other, "one of the most remarkable men in the country." But so he was. They all were.

In all this Lincoln fell into his place. He liked politics better than law and both of them better than business. Of personal fortune he took but

69

little account: kept no books and lived in his pocket with debts as a background.

Stuart went to Congress and the partnership ended in 1841. After that Lincoln was in partnership with Judge Logan for four years: then started an office of his own into which he took as his partner young "Billy" Herndon, son of a Springfield storekeeper. The partnership and the friendship never ended. Later on (1888) Herndon wrote Lincoln's life. It is part of the Lincoln myth to disbelieve what Herndon wrote if it does not square with the imaginary Lincoln. But Herndon was an honest man, and loved and admired and followed Lincoln to the end.

For Lincoln's first ten years in Springfield politics overshadowed law. Such success as he had in his profession did not rest on profound application or profound knowledge, or profound anything. Lincoln was never a great lawyer. His industry came in fits. He subsided on a cracker barrel. But all the world liked him. He could make a farmer jury laugh or cry. He had a quaint self-forgetting honesty that proved good policy. And out of court his unending stories, as broad as they were long, gathered a flock of listeners in the tavern parlor and a cluster of heads at the windows.

All his life Lincoln told stories,—his own or other people's, he was indifferent as to that. The stories, if his own, were mostly parables, quaint applications of daily happenings. He would tell the same story again and again. On the face of it this suggests the familiar type of story-teller who lives by "hearing a good one the other day," and repeating it till he hears another. Lincoln's so-called "stories," gathered into a book, are for the most part pretty dreary. But no doubt the telling of them was another thing. "I have seen him surrounded," writes Herndon, "by a crowd of as many as two and in some cases three hundred people all deeply interested in the outcome of the story. . . . His countenance and his features seemed to take part in the performance. . . . His little gray eyes sparkled: a smile seemed to gather up curtain-like the corners of his mouth: his frame quivered with suppressed excitement; and when the point—or 'nub' of the story as he called it,—came, no one's laugh was heartier than his. . . ."

All this was a wonderful asset for a country lawyer and politician in a rising town in the roaring 'forties.

Then there came into Lincoln's tragic life the added tragedy of his marriage.

In Springfield lived a handsome Kentucky girl called Mary Todd. She was just the opposite of Abraham Lincoln. She was as stylish and self-assured in company as he was shy and rustic. She had a self-will and force of character very attractive in a girl of twenty but destined to ripen into selfish eccentricity in middle age and to subside in her widowhood into sullen imbecility.

She came from a slave state and was all for slavery. Her people had had land and slaves, had been quite prominent in bygone wars and were about as good as anybody. Any one who understands a Mississippi metaphor can place them exactly with the statement that they didn't have to "take back water from anybody."

Mary Todd was socially above Abraham Lincoln.

High flying biographers describe her in such phrases as a "haughty belle," an "aristocrat" of a family of the "bluest blood in Kentucky." But we must write all these down quite a lot. It is the language of another world. Grass, but not blood, is blue in Kentucky. Aristocrats do not square with two-dollar boarding houses, bob-sleighs and frame churches. And in Kentucky they have better things to do than breed aristocrats.

This language only means that Mary Todd came of a richer family than the Lincolns with more style to it, that Mary Todd had lots of nice clothes to wear for nice occasions, and had learned in Evansville what she understood was French.

Lincoln was attracted, was dazzled by Mary Todd. That he ever loved her in any sense worthy of the name, is more than doubtful. His love for Anne Rutledge, his hand-in-hand courtship with her when they sat awkwardly together and talked of marrying and going to college, has in it all of the colors of the morning. His courtship of Mary Todd, his oafish backings and fillings, his mawkish confidences, his advances and retreats have in them the bright hues of the comic supplement. Full of doubt and misgiving, he circled round Mary Todd as he did in 1861 round Fort Sumter. He wanted her but didn't like to go and take her. Then there came the definite betrothal and Lincoln's sudden and comic flight on his first "wedding day" (Jan. 1, 1841).

Nor did Mary Todd ever love Lincoln unless perhaps before she got to know him. But she had got it into her head that he was going to succeed. She had an eccentric idea that he would be president of the United States and said so. With this belief she underwent the supreme humiliation that can be put on any bride-elect: all dressed for the wedding, the guests assembled in her father's handsome frame house in Springfield, the cake, the ring, the jokes, the minister, all set,—and her plighted lover in his new clothes and plug hat hiding somewhere round a tavern.

Such at least is the story written down by Herndon "for twenty years his friend and partner and from first to last his warm admirer." Nor does controversy shake it much. Why doubt it? It all fits together.

Mary Todd "stood for it." She knew what she wanted. There was more advancing and retreating: Lincoln tried to get out of it all: she wouldn't let him Finally she got him duly married (Nov. 4, 1842) and they went to live, at four dollars a week, in a frame boarding house in Springfield. The rest was easy. She had only to wait till Lincoln became president. And she did.

Meantime Lincoln's home life, such as it began, soon crumbled into nothing. He passed his time in the office, in the courts, in the tavern. When the other lawyers hurried home from their circuits in the country towns, eager for the home fires and the faces round them, Lincoln stayed away. "He spent his Sundays," so wrote his law partner later on, "with the loungers at the country tavern, and only went home at the end of the circuit or term of court." "Lincoln himself," says a fellow attorney, Judge Davis, "never had much to say about home, and we never felt free to comment on it. Most of us had pleasant, inviting homes and as we struck out for them I'm sure each one of us down in our hearts had a mingled feeling of pity and sympathy for him."

There were children of the marriage, four little boys, to whom Lincoln was deeply attached. Death was to claim two of them in Lincoln's lifetime. "Eddie" died at Springfield and William in his father's arms in the White House. He never scolded the children nor corrected them. All accounts run the same. He let them do as they pleased.

Such was Abraham Lincoln's home life. It never altered nor improved.

In his early years at Springfield Lincoln took a prominent part, a leading part, in the debates of the legislature of which he was a member till 1843. At times the debates turned on national questions reflected from Washington,—the question of banks versus a government treasury, and the larger question of national improvements. But for much of the rest of the time the legislature talked local politics, voted, intrigued and tricked on party lines. The prohibition question—then called "Temperance" and just gathering force, was a standing topic: so also the repudiation or payment of the state debt, with many minor things, dreary enough in retrospect. For the time the larger issue of slavery had dropped out. The national excitement over the killing of Lovejoy, the abolitionist (in 1837), had died down. "Lincoln," says his admirable biographer, Senator Beveridge, "had seemingly forgotten Lovejoy and was not, at that time, interested in the slavery question." The oratory was that of the "roaring forties." One of Lincoln's chief speeches, reprinted as a campaign document for use in the presidential campaign of 1840 declares, as part of its peroration, that "the great volcano at Washington, aroused and directed by the evil spirit that reigns there, is belching forth the lava of political corruption . . . in a current broad and deep . . . on its bosom are riding, like demons on the waves of hell, the imps of that evil spirit."

Presumably in these roaring times even hell liquefied and came on in waves.

But Lincoln's political activities did not end with his last term in the state legislature. He remained an active member of the Whig party in the locality, his widespread popularity an unfailing asset. His ambition took a higher flight. He aimed at representing in Congress his fellow citizens of the seventh district of Illinois. In two successive elections (1842 and 1844) he worked hard to secure the coveted prize for his friends. Then came Lincoln's turn (1846). These were the good old days of "rotation in office," condemned by all moral and academic authorities, but quite natural to plain people of the rising West. Offices and salaries were too good for any man to have more than his share. The maxim, *ôte-toi de là que je m'y mette,*—spoken in derision by the Emperor Napoleon III,—seemed common sense to the lawyers of Springfield.

Lincoln ran his campaign for the nomination on that ground. He flooded the district with personal letters of appeal. "Turn about is fair play," was the burden, in fact was the very wording, of his plea. Once nominated as a Whig candidate, he had to face as his Democrat rival the Rev. Peter Cartwright, a Methodist preacher. The election left out national issues. Both candidates had the same views on the Texas question, on Oregon, on slavery: so all that was omitted. Lincoln spoke strongly in favor of the opening war with Mexico: he wanted no hesitation from President Polk. But neither did the Rev. Peter Cartwright. So the campaign was made on the personal issues. One side argued that Lincoln, as a notorious infidel, was not fit for Congress, the other that Peter Cartwright, as a minister, was too good for it.

The victory was won by Lincoln's popular appeal. There was no withstanding that. Everybody liked Abraham Lincoln. His great strength, his easy nature, his tolerant mind, his obvious love of all men,—all that, as we say now, "got over" to the people. There is something in the conception of a "kindly giant" that appeals through all ages,—the contrast between power to harm and the will to help. Lincoln never really had an enemy: later in life there were millions of people who vomited out their hate against him, derided, cursed and ridiculed him. But these had never seen and known him. To them he was a name, an incarnation. But for those who knew him in the courts and taverns of his home state, already there was growing up the legend of honest Old Abe—old at forty. This was to ripen into the Father Abraham of the millions of marching men; the measured beat of their footsteps still carrying him on into eternity.

So Lincoln with Mrs. Lincoln and the little boy Robert, now six, went off to Washington. There Lincoln sat in the House of Representatives for his two-year term, an unknown man when he went in, and an unknown man when he came out. There were giants in those day in the Congress: in the

SCENE FROM THE AMERICAN TEMPEST
(*From* PUNCH, *January, 1863*)

Senate, Webster and Calhoun and Cass and Benton and Douglas and Crittenden; in the House, John Quincy Adams, the "grand old man" of the hour; Alexander H. Stephens and Robert Toombs,—men whose names are history. But Lincoln was not yet of these.

The Washington of 1847 was a vast straggling town of about 30,000 people, one-quarter of them colored. It was unkempt, half built, with neither lights nor sewers: with streets all dirt or huge uneven cobblestones. Charles Dickens had seen it five years before and finding it unlike Piccadilly and Paris had swept it scornfully aside. Nor was there yet, among the trees and gardens, back yards and courts overlooked by the wooden dome of the unfinished capitol, much of the vision of the marbled beauty that was to come.

Slaves moved in the streets, and moved, many of them, chained in gangs,—they called them "coffles" of slaves,—market stuff, bought and sold for the South. It was said that the District raised and sold a thousand a year. Thus every member of Congress got his object lesson on slavery.

The huge, slovenly town was a mixture of affluence and poverty, of grandeur and shabbiness. There was a fashionable society with foreign ambassadors and officers to give it tone. Of that Lincoln saw nothing. There were endless boarding houses, half shabby, half genteel, where the members boarded and clubbed together in "messes" for their meals. In such a boarding house lived the Lincolns,—Sprigg's boarding house on Capitol Hill, now replaced by the Library of Congress. We have a first-hand account of their life there in the *Personal Reminiscences* of a certain Dr. Samuel Busey. Lincoln enjoyed the same kind of popularity in his Washington boarding house as he did round the taverns of Illinois. His stories—"some of which," says the doctor, "were very broad"—made a big hit at the mess. When he went to the nearby bowling alley for a game—his only exercise—, a crowd of men and boys gathered to listen,—just as they did at the doors and windows of the taverns. The doctor took to Lincoln, as did all plain men, thought him simple and unpretentious, and said that when the others disputed and quarreled Lincoln made them all laugh and forget it. So would he gladly have done thirteen years later.

But in Congress Lincoln made no hit and attracted no attention. He had nothing to say, nothing that others had not already said with more conviction. In his only speech of magnitude (January 12, 1842) Lincoln sided with the Congress Whigs in attacking the Mexican War, which he had defended to the Illinois Whigs. He brought forward a set of sophistical resolutions about the exact "spot" where the Mexicans first attacked the Americans, and whether the "spot" was or was not in the United States. But when angry men in unknown country start fighting along an unknown border, they leave it to lawyers to worry where the "spot" is. Lincoln's resolutions fell flat in Washington. Beyond a passing retort no notice was taken in Congress and the press was silent. But at home in Illinois there was a furious denunciation.

Lincoln had got in wrong. The home papers reported him talking of a "war of rapine and murder," and spoke of the "blood of poor innocent unoffending people whose only crime was weakness." Perhaps Lincoln said this and perhaps not. Even in the pruned and edited *Congressional Globe,* he spoke of "military glory" as a "rainbow that rises in showers of blood." But the home people had been reading the long lists of the American dead and wounded at Buena Vista and Cerro Gordo and had been reviving their memories of Santa Anna's brutal slaughter of the Texans at the Alamo,—the Ther-

79

mopylæ of America. With the home people "military glory" stood high. They would rather read of Captain Jefferson Davis fighting heroically at the head of the Mississippi rifles, of George B. McClellan, a boy just out of West Point, promoted for bravery on the field, or of stout old Zachary Taylor, the head and hero of the war. The episode ended Lincoln's chance of reëlection.

One interesting passage in the speech, which passed unnoticed at the time, came back at Lincoln years afterwards as a boomerang. In talking of Texas he made what was practically an ideal statement of the academic case for secession.

"Any people anywhere," said Lincoln, "being inclined and having the power have the right to rise up and shake off the existing government, and form a new one that suits them better. Nor is this right confined to cases in which the whole people of an existing government may choose to exercise it. Any portion of such people that can, may revolutionize and make their own of [sic] so much of the territory as they inhabit. More than this, a majority of any portion of such people may revolutionize, putting down a minority, intermingled with or near about them, who may oppose this movement."

It would be hard to find a more direct assertion of the political right of secession. Nor would many people doubt it, within the proper limits of its application, as a right of all of the people, practically all, in a territory truly a unit, and not a part, nor a menace, of another. The real moral issue over Southern secession was that it carried the sin of slavery with it. This was different.

But with the thirtieth congress still sitting and with his term not yet expired Lincoln threw himself into the national presidential campaign of 1848. For the Whigs the main choice was between Henry Clay and General Zachary Taylor. Lincoln from the start rallied to Taylor's support. He had just the qualifications to make him a good candidate. He was a Whig but he came from Louisiana, was a big slaveholder and a war hero without enough education or knowledge of finance to make him offensive to plain people.

The Whig party side-tracked all questions of slavery. It rested on "the broad and firm platform of the constitution" and advocated "peace, prosperity and union."

This was too much for a section of the party which could not tolerate such a platform. They broke away and formed the Free Soil Party with a platform of its own,—slavery where it is now, but no extension of it to free soil,—and above all opposition to the slave power. There was a great drift of the younger Whigs—in Massachusetts a landslide—to the new party. It enlisted the eloquence of Charles Sumner, the family prestige of Charles Francis Adams, the energy of John A. Andrew, the famous "war-governor" of later years. With them were Whittier and Lowell and Longfellow,—bringing the inspiration of art to the new cause.

Lincoln worked hard against them. He sat in the Philadelphia convention that nominated Taylor, worked at Washington under Taylor's national committee, and made a "stump speech" in Congress on the issue (July 2, 1848). He showered the seventh

district of Illinois with letters: he urged the formation of a "Rough and Ready" Club. He used all
the arts and artifices of a "born politician,"—to fight
the principles he was to champion ten years later.

In the campaign Lincoln visited New England.
He had not been solicited as a speaker in the national
campaign. Chance came to him by the failure of
other speakers. He spoke in a mixed meeting at
Worcester, urging the reunion of the party. He
denounced the abolitionists. "I have heard," he said,
"that you have abolitionists here. We have a few
in Illinois and we shot one the other day." This
meant Lovejoy, the martyr to the cause. Other
invitations to speak followed, at Cambridge, at
Lowell and elsewhere, and even at Boston. He
made the same speech with anecdotes and stories
that brought down the house. But he left out Lovejoy. Lincoln's activity was all in vain. Taylor
succeeded but not Lincoln. The Whig party was
visibly dissolving into fragments. With it Lincoln
was washed away.

There followed after the election the "hang-over"
session of the expiring Congress (December, 1848)
in which Lincoln still held a seat. The slave question burst its way into debate. There was an attempt
to introduce a bill to abolish slavery and the slave
trade in the District of Columbia. Lincoln proposed to direct the committee to bring in a bill for
gradual emancipation, with "active and efficient
means to arrest and deliver up to their owners all
fugitive slaves escaping into the district." With that,
Wendell Phillips called Lincoln "the slave hound
from Illinois." The abolitionists turned to rend

82

him. The Whigs were done with him, and the Democrats had never known him.

The Whig administration offered him as a solace the secretaryship of the territory of Oregon. As governor he would have gone: but Mrs. Lincoln refused to go as anything. That settled it. Lincoln went back to Springfield and the law. Politically he was down and out. His father was in distress, begging for twenty dollars. His relatives were poor and clamoring, himself in debt, and of no seeming account to the world. He took it hard, we are told by his law-partner Billy Herndon. "Political defeat wrought a marked effect on him. It went below the skin and made a changed man of him."

Thus Lincoln went into the wilderness to eat bitter bread for five years. But there was still no hatred, no bitterness in his soul, except as against himself.

IV

TOWARDS THE ABYSS

THE Niagara River moves from Lake Erie in a broad, calm flood. It gathers force. The water, still unbroken, runs with increasing speed. It twists and turns in eddies. Foam gathers on the surface. As the miles pass, the water begins to toss in showers of spray and leap and break against the rocks of the river-bed. The speed becomes a rush, the foam a tumult, the sound of the water rising to a roar as it plunges reckless into the abyss. . . .

So runs the allotted course of ten years' history of America, plunging forward to secession.

The Compromise of 1850 settled nothing. The slavery question would not down. In vain the leaders on both sides tried to drop it out of national politics. In vain Senator Douglas declared that he would never make another speech on it. In vain did Congress speak of the "finality" of the settlement. What they took to be the end was only the beginning.

Slavery was becoming with every year the great national issue,--unavoidable. With each year the tumult swelled. The winds of discord rose to a gale. The compromise had "settled" the fugitive slave question by authorizing the full power of the law. The armed force of the nation, under the flag of the Union, must drag the negro back to bondage. Thus was Anthony Burns marched through the streets of Boston, the cradle of liberty (1854) with a regiment of soldiers to keep back the roaring and indignant mob that would have rescued him to freedom.

The fugitive law shocked public feeling. To the abolitionists were now joined the angels of mercy, the plain agents of human sympathy, farm women and their husbands,—helping the run-away slaves across the so-called "free-states"; hiding them in barns; carrying them by night by an "underground railway" of salvation, till the slave was ferried over the boundary to British territory, where his chains fell from him.

The slave question and the sorrows of the slave broke over the boundaries of the nation and reached the ears of the world. In Cincinnati lived a little woman called Mrs. Harriet Beecher Stowe, the harassed mother of a family of six, as poor as only a minister's wife can be. But in the midst of her household cares she wrote for an abolitionist newspaper a serial story called *Uncle Tom's Cabin*. It has become one of the world's books, part of the world's history. It came out as a book in the summer of 1852. Three hundred thousand copies were at once sold in the States. It was translated into all the greater languages of Europe. The tears of thousands—of millions—of little children fell upon the page. For those who read it in the North, in British America and across the sea, a dark shadow fell over the Southern States, shutting out the sunlight from the cornfield. In the apotheosis of the sublime figure of Uncle Tom, beaten to death, reviled and uncomplaining, Mrs. Stowe reconstructed for the docile negro race the martyrdom of Jesus Christ. Unconsciously the book conveyed the impression to its reader that all Southerners were as cruel all the time as one brutal master or overseer might be: that a docile and unoffending race was handed over to the brute tyranny of their mercenary masters.

Mrs. Stowe had never known the South. To the people there her book was a wicked travesty. It set forth isolated crimes and exceptional brutality as the stuff of which their lives were made. But scoff as they might, answer it as they might, they could not unwrite the book. All the world read it with tears, with rising indignation, with contempt.

Years later in the White House Abraham Lincoln met Mrs. Stowe and bent his huge frame to reach to take the worn little hand that had held the pen. "So this," he said, "is the little woman who wrote the book that made the big war."

But soon the fugitive slave question was only a minor part of the issue. All the rest of it was thrown into the shadow by the new and lurid light that rose on the western horizon. The alarm bell of Thomas Jefferson in 1820 was as nothing to the new alarms of flame and tumult in Nebraska.

The compromise had settled, or sidetracked, the question of slavery in Arizona and New Mexico. But the greater question was as to slavery in "Nebraska." This vast region (presently to be called Kansas and Nebraska) was the fertile unoccupied territory that lay west of the Missouri River to the

Rocky Mountains. Thrown open to settlement, it would represent 15,000,000 acres of farm land of wonderful fertility, no forest to clear, waving with prairie grass and waiting for the plow. More than that. The gold rush to California that set in after 1848 was making the Nebraska territory one of the highways of the world. Across it there struggled the long trains of covered wagons and the long troops of mounted men that carried every summer 60,000 new adventurers to the gold country. The new railways (reaching to Chicago in 1852), and the painted steamers of the Mississippi and the Missouri carried the pioneers to the edge of the great plains. At every spot on the route and far out on the plains themselves, were being organized centers of supply, towns staked out where many immigrants settled down rather than go on.

It was a movement that nothing could stop. Population was pouring across the Missouri boundary where slavery ended. What was there to be beyond?

The law had "settled" that question also. When Congress put slavery into Missouri in 1821 it had declared it shut out for the future for any territory as far north as Missouri (north that is of latitude 36° 30′, the southern boundary of the State).

But much that mattered now. With California already admitted (1850) as a free state, the "balance" in the Senate was disturbed. With the Nebraska territory broken into two free states, with more to follow, the cause of slavery, the cause of the South was lost. The Southern leaders spoke of it exactly that way, making no bones about it. They were fully conscious now of where they stood. They spoke heroically, fearlessly,—spoke of the cause of slavery as the French might speak of the soil of France, or the English of the bulwark of the navy.

For the South, Nebraska must be reclaimed for slavery, or the South would be lost. Congress must repeal the law. Congress did. Senator Stephen Douglas, aspiring to national leadership and the presidency, staked his chances on that. He took his stand on a new doctrine of "squatter sovereignty," the sovereignty of the "people on the spot." After long and violent debates he brought about (1854) the repeal of the provisions of the law of 1821 and the opening of Kansas-Nebraska with slavery or freedom, according to which got there first. The result was an inrush of immigrants true and false, "border ruffians" from the Missouri side and Massachusetts "immigrants" carried with the money of the abolitionists. Fighting began at once, with the burning of houses, the murder of settlers and great gatherings of "militia" (meaning men with shotguns and bowie knives), that turned the situation into something like a civil war. Into the fray there threw themselves fierce Southerners like Atchison fighting for what he thought salvation, and sternest of all, John Brown,—hard and Calvinistic, as ruthless as the Old Testament, as vengeful as its God,—coming from Ohio to swing the sword of the Lord in Gideon.

The tumult rose to the very verge of civil war. There were two governments, with two proposed constitutions,—and two "armies" almost at one another's throats. Just in time the national government and the political parties managed to check the situation. The oncoming election of 1856 threw its shadow before. The Democrats—Pierce as President and Jefferson Davis his Secretary of War—dared not alienate the whole of the Northern vote.

But the ashes of the burning houses and the ravaged settlements were still ready to start into a flame.

As if the fugitive slaves and Nebraska were not enough for a harassed nation, a new apple of discord was tossed into the vexed arena. The Minerva who threw it was represented by the emaciated figure and the trembling hand of old Judge Taney, Chief Justice of the United States, and the apple was called the Dred Scott decision of 1857.

The legal situation involved is as intricate as it is unimportant. The plain meaning of the decision was that a slave was "property" in the United States and that his master could take his "property" anywhere where the American flag protected the sacred liberty guaranteed by the constitution. This automatically spread slavery not only over Nebraska but perhaps by implication over Massachusetts.

Such was the situation when Abraham Lincoln came back from the wilderness to the arena of politics. This is not to be regarded as the return of Achilles from his tent, or of Napoleon from Elba. Lincoln—outside of Illinois—was still nobody in particular. But a new emphasis from now on rested on the fact that he was in Illinois. For Illinois was now becoming the storm center of the United States. The northern part of the state was overwhelmingly against slavery, the south—colonized in part from over the Ohio—more doubtful, if not pro-slavery in its sympathy. The state was the center of the activity of Stephen Douglas, and the birthplace and cradle of the new Republican party. For Lincoln opportunity had come.

During these intervening years Lincoln had gone on with his legal practice in Springfield. Round him life moved on, transforming the little town and its environment. At the time when Lincoln came back from Congress it had grown to a place of 4,000 people. When he left it forever (in 1861), the population was almost 10,000. There were plenty of new buildings—the state buildings, factories, churches, hotels. The telegraph by the middle of the century connected the town with Chicago and St. Louis. The railway reached Chicago in 1852 and within four years penetrated the State of Illinois from the Lake to the Mississippi and the Ohio. With the railways came an influx of imported commodities and luxuries, unknown in the pioneer days. People wore different clothes. There were no lawyers in court now in buckskin and moccasins. There were eight daily newspapers in Illinois in 1850. Society had more tone and dress to it and law courts something like decorum.

In all this lived and moved Abraham Lincoln, going on circuit, sleeping in the taverns, telling everlasting stories. He attracted people everywhere, especially the men. He seemed to be that paradoxical thing, an honest lawyer. Endless anecdotes endorse the fact. "Yes," he once said to a client, "there is no reasonable doubt that I can gain your case for you. I can set a whole neighborhood at loggerheads: I can distress a widowed mother and her six fatherless children and thereby get you six hundred dollars, which rightfully belongs, it appears to me, as much to them as to you. I shall not take your case but I will give you a little advice for nothing. You seem a sprightly energetic man. I would advise you to try your hand at making six hundred dollars some other way."

It is Herndon who tells the story. It is of no consequence whether it is true or not: if Lincoln didn't say this, he said a hundred things like it.

It was this that gave him his peculiar place, that raised him from "Lawyer Lincoln" to "Honest Old Abe" and lifted him into the presidency on John Hanks's rails.

Biographers of Lincoln have recorded the fact that on his return to politics he seemed a changed man. His character, as evidenced in his speech and writing, seemed deeper, more serious, more inspired with reality.

Nor need we doubt that this is so. He had had during his years in the wilderness plenty of opportunity for thought. His political failure must have made him take himself to heart, think out what he really believed and look for truth.

Now what did Lincoln really believe? The adherents of Peter Cartwright in the election campaign had called him "an infidel." How did he stand on that? Was Lincoln a Christian,—was he a religious man?

Round this point there has been much controversy, nearly all of it wide of the mark for lack of definition of terms. Lincoln was in the proper sense of the word a deeply religious man. If he had lived in our day he could have called himself a devout Christian, could have belonged to a church. If he had belonged to the Church of England he could have been a bishop, and have preached in St. Paul's.

But in the backwoods generation in North America in which he lived, things were very different; as they still were in the backwoods generation or two which followed and which many of us can still remember. These people, almost without exceptions, were "believers." They took the Bible as they found it and understood it to be true in the plain sense of the word, as they understood words. They thought they learned from it that the world was made out of nothing in six days: two people Adam and Eve, specially created, as the parents of the human race, and with them a set of animals: and afterwards a great many things called "miracles" happened by God's direct intervention to check and contradict the forces of nature. They believed that there is an actual place of great happiness lasting forever, called Heaven: another actual and real place, full of fire, where sinners are burnt forever in actual flames, called Hell. They believed that Christ was not born as mankind are: that he was a God: and that he left this life without death to go direct to Heaven.

The penetrating minds of the present generation enable them to deny all these things and yet remain Christians, and even hold places in the church. But Lincoln's people lacked the insight for that. Overwhelmingly they accepted what seemed the plain truth of the Bible.

But here and there among them was a different man, a questioning man: the more earnestly he sought for reality, the more he questioned. Such a man was apt to find it hard to accept the doctrines of creation, the immaculate conception, the miracles and the resurrection of Christ. Nor had any one yet shown him how to leave them out Such a man was apt to fall into the rôle of the "village atheist," a nineteenth century character whom many of us can remember. Mark Twain was one. Of these some were silent, some combative and scoffing, some harassed with honest doubt: and many deeply religious.

Such a one was Abraham Lincoln.

Lincoln, let it be repeated, was throughout his life an intensely religious man,—if we define religious as apart from creeds and dogmas and churches. In this sense a religious man means a man who lives in the daily consciousness of the transience of life and the imminence of death. Such a feeling carries with it a supreme sense of duty, and a sense of tolerance towards all men. It leaves no time for anger and for hatred. Time is too short.

On Lincoln had fallen early in life the full bitterness of death. As a child he had helped to make from rude slabs the coffin of his mother. Later he had known the grief of a father who held to his breast the dead body of a child, inert and still, the passion of sorrow over death with no consolation beyond the dumb dignity of despair.

But all this and these feelings were quite apart from "religion" as known in Springfield a century ago.

Lincoln, it is true, was a close and constant reader of the Bible. It was one of the books from which he had learned to read. There were verses of it that he loved all his life, because he had learned them from his mother's lips before his hand or eye could understand the written word. It was no affectation, no effect of oratory that led him to cast his greater speeches in the firm strong mold of the biblical thought and phrase.

But Lincoln did not "believe the Bible," as they did, or said they did, in Springfield a hundred years ago. He didn't believe in stories of men in whales' bellies, in miracles over fire and water, in birth direct from the Holy Ghost and in a fierce and angry God trampling down his slaughtered victims and visiting the sins of the fathers on the children.

If this meant being an "infidel," Lincoln was an infidel. He wrote while a young man a little pamphlet or essay to show that Christ was not the son of God. Herndon says that one of his friends burnt the manuscript of the essay for fear it might get published and do Lincoln harm. John Stuart, Lincoln's first law-partner, says that "he was an open and avowed infidel and went further against Christian beliefs and doctrines and principles than any man I ever heard." Herndon gives abundant testimony.

Lincoln's lack of "religion" seems to have been an accepted fact to those about him in Springfield. His wife took a church pew. Lincoln stayed away. In Washington in his Congress days he never went to church.

In Lincoln's speeches, even the earlier ones, are found many phrases that seemed to be based on earnest religious belief. But such expressions as these are, in part at least, merely the stock in trade of the politician, a mere lip service to current and established religion. Solemn and sanctimonious references to the Providence that is guiding him fall easily from the politician's lips. He scarcely knows where belief ends and humbug begins. He falls into an easy alliance with "Providence." It enhances his own dignity.

But in Lincoln's case the utterances had from the start an undercurrent of reality: in the end they became intense and earnest. It is true that John Nicolay, later, along with John Hay, Lincoln's secretary, wrote to Herndon after Lincoln's death (May 27, 1865) to say, "Mr. Lincoln did not to my knowledge in any way change his religious ideas, opinions, or beliefs from the time he left Springfield to the day of his death. I do not know just what they were, never having heard him explain them in detail."

What happened was not a change but an intensification; and it had no connection with churches and miracles and the rantings of itinerant preachers. In the loneliness of his great office, in the isolation of his responsibility, Lincoln turned to God. It was as God's instrument that he freed the slaves: he knew it.

But all this was later on.

Meantime Lincoln was back in politics, reappear-

ing on the stump in the congressional campaign of
1854. His ideas were still half formed, and in conflict with his inner self. But even at that, there was
a new force and power, and a new earnestness in
Lincoln that rapidly raised him to a new place. He
was no longer merely "playing politics." Nor were
any of the leaders. The current of national life was
beginning to run too fiercely for that. The Kansas-
Nebraska tumult showed the issues to be those of
life and death, of national salvation or disaster.

One of the speeches—made at the State Fair of the
autumn of 1854—in answer to one by Senator Douglas, carried far. Lincoln spoke straight out on the
question of slavery.

He spoke of the "monstrous injustice of slavery."
He denied that there can be moral right in the en-
slaving of one man by another. He poured out
against slavery all the contempt and loathing that
words can convey. But when he had said all that,
he concluded with a strong plea against interfering
with it.

"Let us," he said, "return it to the position our
fathers gave it and there let it rest in peace. Let
us readopt the Declaration of Independence and the
practices and policies which harmonize with it. Let
North and South, let all Americans, let all lovers
of liberty everywhere form in the great and good
work. If we do this, we shall not only have saved
the Union, but we shall have so saved it as to make
it and keep it forever worthy of the saving. We
shall have so saved it that the succeeding millions
of free, happy people, the world over, shall rise up
and call us blessed to the latest generation."

Observe the hopeless inconsistency of the argument! Slavery is good enough for the 5,000,000 people of the South. On their hands the chains are to stay forever, as their part of the Declaration of Independence. Lovers of liberty even in foreign countries are to witness and admire forever the continuation of their bondage.

Slavery is good enough for a quarter of a continent, good from the Potomac to the Rio Grande. But if a group of the happy people of the South propose to go out into empty Arizona with a group of their happy slaves and found a new home as good as South Carolina and as happy as Virginia,—then that is a hideous moral wrong.

The argument cannot stand; and in his soul Lincoln must have known it, even if his brain had not yet puzzled it out. The Southern doctrine, "slavery is a good thing, the more we have of it the better," is a perfectly logical and consistent proposition. Its value turns on the question of fact, whether slavery *is* or is *not* a good thing. But Lincoln's argument is trash: and he was soon to amend it.

Trash or not, it took effect and carried far. In Illinois, though not yet with the nation at large, Lincoln was a marked man. They wanted him for the senate,—either to rival Stephen Douglas by being chosen in 1856, or by ousting Douglas whose term was to expire in 1858.

There followed the presidential campaign and election of 1856. The Whigs made a feeble appearance only to be washed out of sight, carrying only one state,—the end of the party. The real struggle was between the Democrats and the new Republican party, now nationally organized (Feb. 22, 1856) under that name. The Democrats put up James Buchanan, elderly and colorless, chosen on the seventeenth ballot; the Republicans General John Frémont, a pioneer hero of California, chosen in a single shout of applause. The Democrats won, carrying with them the vote of the solid South, a new thing in American politics, destined to remain for two generations.

Lincoln played a conspicuous part. He had cut loose from the Whig party. He had missed the party nomination for the senatorship of 1856, but his influence was decisive in beating the Democrats for the prize. But for Lincoln that was the end of the Whigs. Reluctantly he went over to the new Republican party, a prominent adherent from the start. He sat in the (first) Republican national convention (at Philadelphia). There he made a speech, the text of which is lost, but which enjoys the prestige of all lost speeches. He campaigned his State. His speeches which survive only in fragments reiterate his territorial argument.

The Republicans lost. But the defeat was as pregnant with future victory as the victory of their opponents ominous of defeat. They carried Ohio and New York and, excepting Maine, the whole of New England.

The current of national life moved faster and faster, carrying Lincoln on the crest. Following on the presidential election of 1856 came the national excitement over the final decision of the Supreme

Court in 1857 in the case of the negro Dred Scott. The famous case had been in the courts since 1852. Its details and its ramifications would fill a volume. But the essential part of it centered round the plain question whether a slave was still a slave if taken by his master into one of the territories. Judge Taney said that he was and needlessly added his brutal dictum "that the negro has no rights which the white man is bound to respect."

This decision annihilated the fortunes of Senator Douglas. It established those of Abraham Lincoln. Douglas's fundamental platform that the people in the territory had a natural "squatter sovereignty" and could decide for themselves, was rent asunder by the decision. Douglas tried in vain to patch up a lame argument to the effect that if people in a territory don't want slavery they could kill it by unfriendly legislation. This only meant that people placed in power can circumvent both the constitution and the law by not carrying them out.

For Lincoln the decision meant a flat challenge, something to fight for. It helped the Republican party by virtually denying that such a party could exist. Republicanism leaped triumphantly to new life. Buchanan himself said that the decision, if made in 1856, would have elected Frémont.

Meantime Lincoln and Douglas, now two rival giants in Illinois, belabored one another in speeches and debate.

Douglas made a notable speech in Springfield on June 27, 1857. He tried to show that the Dred Scott decision "firmly established" popular sovereignty and self-government. This sophistical nonsense Lincoln easily tore in pieces in an answering speech.

Back and forward the controversy went. It undermined Douglas as a national leader. He could not adhere to the now triumphant doctrine of territorial slavery, and maintain his own doctrine of people's rights, and with it placated Northern sentiment. He was trying to ride three animals at once, the Northern horse and the Southern mule and the Western mustang. He was destined to fall in a cloud of dust among the three.

But Lincoln was now carrying his argument one stage further. The "happy millions" of his former speech was now exchanged for the idea of "ultimate extinction." Put up at the Republican convention of 1858 as the party's choice for the senatorship, he made a speech which became henceforth the central thread in the fabric of his thought; reiterated again and again on the platform and in the press, and still carrying its echo as part of our common memory of his life.

"Mr. President and Gentlemen of the convention," so spoke Lincoln on June 16, 1858, at Springfield. "If we could first know where we are and whither we are tending, we could better judge what to do, and how to do it. We are now far into the fifth year since a policy was initiated with the avowed object and confident promise of putting an end to slavery agitation. Under the operation of that policy, that agitation has not only not ceased, but has constantly augmented. In my opinion it will not cease until a crisis shall have been reached and passed. 'A house divided against itself cannot stand.' I believe this government cannot endure permanently half slave and half free. I do not expect the Union to be dissolved,—I do not expect the house to fall,—but I do expect it will cease to be divided. It will become all one thing or all another. Either the opponents of slavery will arrest the further spread of it, and place it where the public mind shall rest in the belief that it is in the course of ultimate extinction; or its advocates will push it forward till it shall become alike lawful in all the States, old as well as new, North as well as South."

This famous sentiment, with its striking biblical phrase, "a house divided against itself cannot stand,"—has since gone round the world. Lincoln reiterated it, and when challenged with it read it out again, flatly and defiantly.

Yet what did he mean with it? When was this "ultimate extinction" to come? Then and later Lincoln would have kept slavery in the States. Even as President he was willing to amend it into the constitution forever,—forever,—as far as human law and human promise could make it. If this was "ultimate extinction" it was far, far away. Was the phrase anything more than resonant oratory? It undoubtedly was. It came from Lincoln's soul. He was torn between his passion for peace and good will, and his passion of anger against slavery. His soul, though he didn't know it, was also a house divided against itself.

That summer, while the senatorial campaign was on, there occurred the far-famed Lincoln-Douglas debates, carried out by joint arrangement at various Illinois centers in July and August of 1858.

These Lincoln-Douglas debates have been lifted by the retrospect of history out of all proportion to what they meant to the nation at the time, and out of all proportion of what they ought to mean. Their interest exists because it was Lincoln who spoke, but Lincoln was not Lincoln then. Let those who will, read the speeches and judge for themselves. They may all be found set out in full in the volume of the *Complete Works* of Abraham Lincoln as edited by Nicolay and Hay. The opinion may be hazarded that the great bulk of it all is dreary stuff, and the arguments, as read, today, prolonged, sophisticated and wearisome.

Nor need we attach too much importance to the fact that the people from all quarters "flocked to hear them"; that the farmers and their wives and families, on foot, on horseback and in wagons, an army of picnickers on the march gathered from all points of the compass. It meant but little. In those prairie days there was so little to flock to, so little to vary the crude life of the farm and the frontier, that people gathered gladly in crowds for anything or everything that broke the stern monotony of existence. A revival camp-meeting, with an itinerant preacher foaming at the mouth, drew a great concourse. John Hay tells us that when Vannoy, the wife-murderer, was to be executed at Springfield "whole families put on their best clothes and drove fifty miles through bottomless mud and swollen rivers to see him hanged." "How barren of incident," says the same writer, "was the life of these obscure founders of a great empire. Any subject of conversation, any cause of sensation was a godsend."

As a matter of fact similar great picnic crowds had turned out at various political gatherings in the slavery campaign of the decade of the 'fifties.

AN HEIR TO THE THRONE,
OR THE NEXT REPUBLICAN CANDIDATE
(A Currier & Ives print of 1860)

The only note of the sound of the debates that echoes through history is Lincoln's defiant reiteration of his thought and of his words, that a "house divided against itself cannot stand," and of his prophecy of "ultimate extinction." This now carried far, and many people connect its utterance with the Lincoln-Douglas debates. But, as already said, it first belongs elsewhere.

Lincoln lost the senatorial contest. Douglas went back to the Senate. But Lincoln's higher aim,—he declared it such,—was achieved. Douglas could never be president.

Lincoln had risen now to something close to a national reputation. His friends talked already of putting his name up for the Republican convention of 1860. The moving current ran fast and faster and carried Lincoln to success. John Brown's attempt at a slave insurrection (Oct. 16, 1859) appalled the nation. It was necessary to cleanse the new Republican party from the abolitionist stain. Lincoln was called to New York and spoke in the Cooper Institute (Feb. 27, 1860). In this speech there is no word of a house divided against itself, no ominous prophecy of ultimate extinction. The first half of it is an attempt at the legal proof of the right of Congress to control slavery in the territories if it wants to: following that comes an extended argument to show that Republicans are not "Black," that John Brown was not a Republican and that Republicans were not dangerous.

"We declare our belief that slavery is wrong," said Lincoln, "but the slaves do not hear us declare even this. For anything we say or do, the slaves would scarcely know that there is a Republican party." This reassuring statement was followed by a further assurance in conclusion: "Wrong as we think slavery is, we can yet afford to let it alone where it is because that much is due to the necessity arising from its actual presence in the nation."

The speech was a great success. It helped to make Lincoln known in the East; and it marked him as a "safe" man. Readers of today must weigh and measure it for themselves; the doctrine that wrong, inflicted on other, humbler people must be tolerated for the sake of the peace and happiness of those whose collective power inflicts it, is and was, for certain consciences, a hard saying. And among such consciences was Lincoln's own.

Speeches followed, in the same tenor, at Hartford (March 5), New Haven (March 6), and Norwich (March 9). "Slavery," said Lincoln, "is wrong,— a great moral wrong" (New Haven). He compared it to "a venomous snake" (Hartford). But of its "ultimate extinction" he said not a word.

Then followed the Republican National Convention held in Chicago (May 16-18, 1860). Its platform voiced the now familiar Republican creed,— slavery where it is, but no further extension. The selection of the candidate was a more doubtful matter. In spite of Lincoln's increasing notoriety, his popular appeal as "Honest Old Abe" and his claim as a man of Illinois, his "availability" as a pioneer and a rail splitter, he was still outranked in the counsels of the party by William H. Seward, former governor of New York and a senator of the United States. Seward's Republicanism was of earlier date. The bold challenge of his phrase,—the "irrepressible conflict,"—had echoed through the nation. But the conventions and the people had grown used to the repeated balloting and the shifting and sifting of votes that cast out the mighty,—the Websters and the Clays, and exalted the unknown as the Pierces and the Polks. Seward, not far from a majority lead on the first vote, was cast aside, and Lincoln nominated for the candidate.

Meantime the Democratic party, unable to agree in convention after fifty-seven ballotings (Charleston, April 25, 1860) adjourned (Baltimore, June 18-28) and broke asunder with two sections of the party under two candidates, Senator Douglas, with half a slave platform and most of the voters, and Breckenridge with a whole platform and only some of the voters. In between stood a compromise party (the Constitutional Union) splitting the vote still further.

There followed the fierce and violent campaign of the summer of 1860, with the open threat of secession. In November Lincoln, with a minority of the people's votes (1,866,352 out of 4,676,858) was chosen for the presidency.

On which, South Carolina in convention shouted and cheered itself out of the Union (Dec. 20, 1860) and the gulf States followed.

V

SECESSION

ABRAHAM LINCOLN, then, through the selection of the electors of the Republican party pledged to vote for him,—was chosen President of the United States,—November 6, 1860. It was, as said, a minority election. Lincoln received 1,866,352 popular votes. The other candidates, put together, received 2,410,501. In the states of Alabama, Arkansas, Florida, Georgia, Louisiana, Mississippi, North Carolina, South Carolina (still nominating by the legislature), Tennessee and Texas, Lincoln did not poll a single citizen's vote. This made his election entirely sectional and obviously out of harmony with national welfare. The Republican party platform had reaffirmed (sec. 4) the principle of slavery,—"the right of each state to order and control its own domestic institutions." It declared itself "to hold in abhorrence all schemes of disunion," denounced as a "dangerous political heresy . . . the new dogma that the constitution carries slavery into any or all the territories of the United States" and declared that "the normal condition of all the territory of the United States is that of freedom." Of the other parties, the Douglas Democrats, calling themselves the "Democracy of the Union," made a platform which took for granted slavery in the slave States, left slavery in the territories to the decision of the courts of law, and denounced the "enactments of State legislatures to defeat the faithful execution of the fugitive slave law." But before the platform was voted the bulk of the Southern delegates had withdrawn. This Democratic party polled a popular vote of 1,375,157 but a vote of only 12 in the electoral college. The Constitutional Union party, which nominated John Bell of Tennessee, emerging out of the crisis itself, stood for "the constitution of the country, the union of the States, the enforcement of the laws": it received 587,830 popular votes with 39 in the electoral college.

The extreme Democrats, the Southern party, *par excellence,* declared for the right of all citizens "to settle with their property in the territories" (this meant automatic slavery) and denounced the attempts to defeat the faithful execution of the fugitive slave law. On union their platform was ominously silent. Their popular vote was 847,514, their electoral vote 72. Thus Lincoln when the electoral return was duly counted on Feb. 13, 1861, had 180 out of 303 votes.

Let it be noted that all of these parties stood openly and firmly for slavery. Even in the Republican platform there was no question raised of moral wrong, of ultimate extinction. They endorsed slavery for an area of nearly 1,000,000 square miles and a population of 10,000,000 people. They only cut it from the back settlements, the open plains on the frontier of the North and West, where it was little likely in any case to spread. This acceptance of slavery was reiterated by all the leaders and speakers of the party and it was put as the foremost thought of Lincoln's inaugural address and in his offer to nail slavery to the mast by a constitutional amendment. It is hard for those who feel that the very idea of human slavery is repellent to our moral sense, to see anything heroic in this. Such of the heroic and the ideal as was there, lay not in the declared policy of the party but in the minds of vast numbers of its adherents, who had grown to hate the shame and the sting of slavery and wanted, in their hearts, to be done with it.

These factors in the situation misled and confused public opinion abroad. If Lincoln and all his associates, and presently his government, emphatically declared that they stood for slavery in the slave States, the surrender of fugitive slaves and the right of the master to own his slave, and that they would rivet it down with an unalterable amendment to bind the future,—how could people in England view the quarrel as a great conflict between slavery and freedom? As yet it was only the twilight of a dawning day.

There followed after the election that interregnum from November to March which was the structural weakness of the American Constitution. Administration moves on like transit on a bridge about to fall.

The outgoing President, James Buchanan, a Northern Democrat, almost seventy years old, only wanted to depart in peace. He would not lift a hand to stay the moving current of events. After him the deluge. South Carolina had seceded from the Union, calling on the Southern States to follow. Convention followed convention. By the first of February, 1861, Mississippi, Florida, Alabama, Georgia, Louisiana, and Texas had voted themselves out of the Union.

Delegates met at Montgomery and formed the new republic of the Confederate States. Their constitution was openly and honestly based on slavery, —the "negro's natural and normal condition." There was nothing of the evasive language of the constitution of 1789 which uses a dozen words to avoid the shame of one.

With that, the flag of the Union was hauled down, its property and its offices taken over, its docks and arsenals seized, its buildings appropriated, its money sequestrated, its authority derided and defied. For all this, Buchanan did nothing. He let the Southern delegates come and go. He carried the mails and handed the Southerners their letters.

The conjectures of history are as idle as they are interesting. To ask what would have happened if things had been otherwise, violates the logic of facts, and the sequence of existing things. But one cannot resist the query, What would have happened if Buchanan had acted in 1860 as Jackson had? One man, at least, in Buchanan's cabinet, showed the Jackson spirit. John Dix, later General Dix of the war, taking over the Treasury when Buchanan's Southerners went out, sent out an order (Jan. 29, 1861), "If any man attempts to haul down the

American flag, shoot him on the spot." The North thrilled for a moment. There were others ready to follow the lead. But Buchanan remained inert and motionless: and Congress crawled on its knees. The flag was hauled down everywhere.

War, let us admit, on a certain scale and of a certain duration, was inevitable. But could it not have been a far lesser war than the appalling conflict that followed? Yet in that case would the war perhaps have passed like a summer storm and left slavery still standing when it was gone? In that case all the passivity of Buchanan, and the indecisions and ineptitudes of Lincoln seem but a part of that final judgment of the Lord as visioned in Lincoln's second inaugural address.

In any case there is no doubt the separation of South from North was made with reluctance, with hesitation, with pain. There was "union sentiment" almost everywhere. People did not so easily forget the memories of the Revolution, their century of Union allegiance, the glories of 1776, and the burden and heat of the hard days of the past, borne willingly together. Secession, at the best, is the tearing asunder of a body, the stifling of a soul. The motive power, be it admitted, was great. It sprang from the hatreds engendered in twenty years of bitter conflict. It was strengthened by the aspirations of politicians, the lust of power. It was nurtured on fears of the future, and to a great extent it was fanned to a flame by the eagerness for material gain, the curse of organized mankind. The Southerners saw in the new Confederacy the hope of new wealth, of a vast commerce, trading freely over the sea with England as a partner, with every Southern port an emporium, and Charleston as the jewel of the Atlantic. All this swept South Carolina forward with hardly a dissenting whisper, and with it the States along the gulf. Yet there were hesitations and backward glances and lingering regrets. In Georgia the sentiment for union, or at least the affection for the Union, was still strong. The State had returned a "Union" majority in the election of November. Leaders in the State, such as B. H. Hill and Alexander H. Stephens, called themselves "Union men" to the very verge of secession. Then Senator Thomas Cobb, anticipating the methods of today, supplied a "formula" which ran, "We can make better terms out of the Union than in it." This, claimed Mr. Stephens afterwards, carried the State out.

In Texas the aged governor Sam Houston—the legendary hero of the State—came out against secession. But his opposition was mingled with vague ideas of a "Lone Star State," an old man's dream of the past. He was swept aside in the movement and deposed. Yet he swore no allegiance to the Confederate States, nor was Texas in the original Montgomery convention.

Greatest of all was the opposition in Virginia. Here Union sentiment was widespread if not universal. It had behind it all the prestige of history, the pride of a State which more than any other except Massachusetts, had made the United States. It could not forget the memory of Washington and Jefferson and Patrick Henry. Virginia had refused to join in the conference proposed by South Carolina in the winter before the election. It had passed Lincoln by, with only 1,929 popular votes in a total of 166,223: but the other votes showed a majority of some 16,000 for the Union candidates. When a convention assembled (Feb. 4, 1861) it was a perplexed gathering: but the Union men claimed a majority of three to one. The State voted money and drilled troops, but not even the fierce partisanship of Governor Letcher could drag it out of the old Union. When Buchanan went out, the stars and stripes still flew on both sides of the Potomac.

So with North Carolina. In January of 1860 an irregular crowd of militia and citizens seized the United States posts (Fort Johnston and Fort Caswell). The Governor gave them back. The legislature voted to call a convention, the citizens voted not to hold it. The State sent emissaries to Montgomery and emissaries to Washington. "The plain people," wrote John Hay, "clung to the Union." The State, under Buchanan's régime, had still not "gone out."

Nor had Arkansas. The election to a convention made early in 1861 showed a "Union vote" of 23,000 against 17,000. A secession ordinance was voted down by 39 to 35 votes. When Lincoln became President, Arkansas was still in the Union.

But in all the states along the sea and the gulf and the river, the intrigue, the effort, the interest, of the politicians, the ruling class, was bent toward secession. The people,—or at least the great masses of them, hung back,—reluctant.

Meantime, during this critical winter of 1860-1861, Abraham Lincoln sat in his office in Springfield, and received and answered letters. So many letters came that presently he had to hire two young men as secretaries,—a new thing for him. Of these, one was John G. Nicolay, a local German-American journalist-editor of education and culture. The other was "Johnny" Hay, a youth of pioneer origin but with the polish of Brown University. He it was who wrote the *Pike County Ballads*. But in later years he recovered sufficient dignity to be the famous John Hay of Theodore Roosevelt's cabinet and of the Panama Canal treaty. When Lincoln had been dead for over twenty years (1886) Nicolay and Hay wrote his biography, framed as a history of the time. Apart from its documents the book is a panegyric and an epic of the North: all Southerners are "traitors" and Lee the biggest of them,—"guilty of desertion and treason." One must measure the famous book by that. Nicolay and Hay are hostile witnesses, their evidence only valid in one direction.

The most important part of Lincoln's correspondence is concerned with the making of his cabinet,—a task which he began on the very night of his election.

Here he needed no teaching. His experience as a politician showed him what to do. He invited into the cabinet all the balanced elements of his support. For Secretary of State he chose William H. Seward, the great Republican leader who had beaten him 173 to 102 on the opening ballot of the convention. With him were invited Simon Cameron and Salmon

Chase and Edward Bates,—also Lincoln's convention rivals. He balanced these Republicans against Union Democrats,—Welles and Caleb Smith and Blair of Maryland. He balanced the West against the East. He even tried to throw into the scale a final touch of Southern weight. This proved impossible.

To John A. Gilmer of Louisiana, one of the Southern possibilities for the cabinet, Lincoln wrote (Dec. 15, 1860) to say that it was not necessary for him to make a new public statement of his views and intentions.

"Carefully read," he said, "pages 18, 19, 74, 75, 88, 89 and 267 of the volume of joint debates between Senator Douglas and myself, with the Republican platform adopted at Chicago and all your questions will be substantially answered." (Presumably Gilmer, in the languor of a Southern plantation, had lots of time for reading.) "I have no thought of advocating the abolition of slavery in the District of Columbia nor the slave-trade among the slave states. . . . I never have been, am not now, and probably never shall be in a mood of harassing the people either North or South. . . . On the territorial question I am inflexible. In this there is a difference between you and us. You think slavery is right and ought to be extended: we think it is wrong and ought to be restricted."

This had become the familiar Lincoln doctrine. It is hard to find it heroic. Turn the last sentence round and it stands: "You think slavery is right and you propose to keep it. We think slavery is wrong and yet we won't try to end it." Of the two the

115

Southerner, if he was honest, had the better case with his conscience.

For greater clearness Lincoln added, "As to the state laws,—if any of them are in conflict with the fugitive slave clause . . . I certainly shall be glad of their repeal."

Writing to Seward,—"private and confidential," Feb. 1, 1861, he says,—"As to fugitive slaves, District of Columbia, slave trade among the slave-states, and whatever springs of necessity from the fact that the institution is amongst us, *I care but little* (italics not Lincoln's), so that what is done is comely and not altogether outrageous. Nor do I care much about New Mexico if further extension be hedged about."

It is a far cry from these sentiments to the sublime language of the Second Inaugural Address. Where do these fetters and manacles and chains, these hunted slaves and sales down the river,—every item of it implied in Lincoln's words,—fit in with the "two hundred and fifty years of the bondsman's un-requited toil," the "Blood drawn by the lash," and the "judgments of the Lord"?

But the great bulk of Lincoln's letters were sent to the innumerable people,—politicians, candidates, business men who wrote to learn his views and what he proposed to do about the impending crisis. All of Lincoln's answers (*Abraham Lincoln: Complete Works: Comprising Speeches, Letters, State Papers and Miscellaneous Writings,* 1907) are framed in the same way. He practically refers his correspondents to the Chicago platform,—the accepted gospel of Republicanism.

To Congressman Kellogg of Illinois he wrote (Dec. 11, 1860): "Entertain no proposition for a compromise in regard to the extension of slavery. . . . You know I think the fugitive-slave law in the constitution ought to be enforced."

There can be no doubt that as the winter months went by, bringing Lincoln nearer and nearer to the great crisis, there came over him more and more the great sense of the awful responsibility laid upon him. And with it came that sense of isolation from human help, because he was to be placed in power above it,—the loneliness that drew Lincoln month by month from the things that he knew were those of man—the arts and wiles of politics—to what he began to feel was God. The "village atheist" was to turn to the man who walked with God. Without this interpretation the sublime faith of the Second Inaugural is blasphemy.

More and more we can see this element in his mind asserting itself, forcing its way towards recognition. It was to be with him in all the perplexities of his ignorance, in the anguish of his indecision, in his pleadings for advice, till it broke its way into the sunlight of his proclamation for which he needed the advice or counsel of no man. This is the real Lincoln, beside which the familiar myth of his sagacity and shrewdness and knowledge of himself and his purpose, is cheap and tawdry.

Nowhere is this better seen than in his closing hour at Springfield. It had been arranged that Lincoln should leave Springfield on February 11, 1861; that he should visit some of the great cities of the

East, and thence to Washington well in time for his inauguration.

It was on a stormy winter morning of driving snow that Lincoln left his home, never to return. He stood in the waiting room of the dingy little railway station, where his friends filed past him one by one with a silent pressure of his hand. Then, in the very moment of departure, his gaunt figure was seen on the platform of the car, his hand raised to hold the attention of the crowd.

John Hay, standing near him, tells us that the words that were spoken seemed like "the tragic shadow of forecasting fate."

"My friends," said Lincoln, "no one, not in my situation, can appreciate my feeling of sadness at this parting. To this place, and the kindness of these people I owe everything. Here I have lived a quarter of a century, and have passed from a young to an old man. Here my children have been born, and one is buried. I now leave, not knowing when or whether ever I may return, with a task before me greater than that which rested upon Washington. Without the assistance of that Divine Being who ever attended him, I cannot succeed. With that assistance, I cannot fail. Trusting in Him, who can go with me, and remain with you, and be everywhere for good, let us confidently hope that all will yet be well. To His care commending you, as I hope in your prayers you will commend me, I bid you an affectionate farewell."

In fancy one can imagine, a shrouded figure, standing beside Lincoln as he spoke,—to take him away,—forever. For he never came back. Perhaps he knew it. The reference to his God, to whose guidance he commends himself, is no longer the lip-service of the politician. It marks the beginning of that new isolation, the loneliness of place and power, above human authority, beyond human help, that was to bring Lincoln into his own.

On his indirect journey to Washington Lincoln stopped to speak at the leading cities,—at Indianapolis, at Cincinnati, at Columbus, at Pittsburgh, at Cleveland, in the chief places in New York State, in the metropolis itself, at Philadelphia and at Harrisburg.

In these last two cities Lincoln was to learn something of the grim realities that now surrounded him. At Philadelphia those about him told him that there was a plot against his life. His journey had been planned and announced as from Philadelphia to Harrisburg and thence by Baltimore to Washington. In Baltimore he was to be killed. Lincoln was told this by the railroad executives, by Allan Pinkerton, their detective, and by a warning letter from General Winfield Scott, the aged commander of the army.

So Lincoln's plan and route were changed. To use the phrase of Goldwin Smith, he "stole by night into the capital." A special train took him to Philadelphia. The telegraph wires were disconnected. Lincoln passed through Baltimore in the night, unrecognized.

A European king, with the Sarajevo spirit, would have gone straight on. European kings hold their kingship on that tenure.   Not so Lincoln.   "A man of less courage," wrote John Hay, "would have shrunk from what must inevitably appear to the public as sign of timidity."   But for that Lincoln cared nothing.   Nor had he any fear of death,— none.   He lived under the shadow and in the prescience of it,—his lot determined, moving on towards his fate.

Plot or not, Lincoln reached Washington.   The South jeered.   The episode was over.

There followed on a gusty spring day of mingled sun and shadow (March 4, 1861) the inauguration of Abraham Lincoln as President of the United States.   As he rode in an open carriage beside the outgoing President, Buchanan, from Willard's Hotel to the Capitol, there were "uncommon precautions to ensure public order."   Double files of a squadron of cavalry rode beside the carriage; sappers and miners marched in front; infantry men and riflemen followed behind.   Squads of riflemen were placed on the housetops to shoot down any one who should fire on the Lincolns from the windows.   Commanding the approach to the Capitol, was old General Scott with a battery of flying artillery.   But all went well.

Beside Lincoln on the platform at the ceremony was the aged Chief Justice Taney, frail and broken with domestic affliction, a withered figure, corresponding in his "fatefulness" though not in appearance, to Helen of Troy.

Here also was Senator Douglas, Lincoln's bygone rival in Illinois, representing at the ceremony the

Congress of the United States. These two and
Buchanan and many others were familiar figures to
the crowd. But for most, for nearly all of them,
this was their first sight of the new President. Apart
from his great height, almost too great for majesty,
Lincoln cut but a poor figure to the eye. Herndon
gives us a picture of the scene, taken he says, from
the words of an eye-witness.

"The tall, gaunt form of the President-elect was
visible, slowly making his way to the front. . . .
He was raising a crop of whiskers of the blacking-
brush variety, coarse, stiff and ungraceful: and in
so doing spoiled or at least seriously impaired, a face
which, though never handsome, had in its original
state, a peculiar power and pathos. On the present
occasion the whiskers were reënforced by brand-
new clothes from top to toe; black dress-coat, instead
of the usual frock, black cloth or satin vest, black
pantaloons and a glossy hat evidently just out of
the box. To cap the climax of novelty, he carried
a huge ebony cane, with gold head the size of an
egg. In these, to him, strange habiliments, he
looked so miserably uncomfortable that I could not
help pitying him. Reaching the platform his dis-
comfort was visibly increased by not knowing what
to do with hat and cane; and so he stood there, a
target for ten thousand eyes, holding cane in one
hand and hat in the other, the very picture of helpless embarrassment. . . . Douglas, who fully took in
the situation, came to the rescue of his old friend
and rival, and held the precious hat until the owner
needed it again. . . . The oath of office was ad-
ministered by Chief Justice Taney, whose black

robes, attenuated figure, and cadaverous countenance reminded me of a galvanized corpse. Then the President came forward and read his inaugural address in a clear and distinct voice."

This inaugural address is one of the major documents of American history. Lincoln had worked upon it line by line, had submitted it, humbly enough, to Seward for suggestions both as to matter and language.

In the address Lincoln reiterates the assertions and the promises of the Chicago platform and the now familiar doctrine of non-interference. "I have no purpose," so he quoted himself, from former speeches, "directly or indirectly, to interfere with the institution of slavery in the States where it exists. I believe I have no lawful right to do so, and I have no inclination to do so." He pledges himself to carry out the fugitive slave law: he cites the provision of the constitution: he tries to brush aside the controversy as to the seizure and surrender of slaves by the State law and by the courts of the States to which they escape, or the seizure and surrender by the action of the national government. "If the slave is to be surrendered," said Lincoln, "it can be of little consequence to him or to others by which authority it is done."

Lincoln goes on to declare that "Union of these States is perpetual": he indicates "the declared purpose of the Union that it will constitutionally defend and maintain itself." But he will not use force. "In doing this there need be no bloodshed or violence; and there shall be none unless it is forced upon the national authority. The power confided

in me will be used to hold, to occupy and to possess
the property and places belonging to the government, and to collect the duties and imposts: but beyond what may be necessary for these objects there
will be no invasion, no using of force against or
among the people anywhere. Where hostility to
the United States shall be so great and so universal
as to prevent competent resident-citizens from holding the Federal offices, there will be no attempt to
force obnoxious strangers among the people for that
object."

Lincoln went on to say that "the mails unless
repelled, will continue to be furnished in all parts
of the Union." As a matter of fact, he went on
furnishing them till the month of June. The
Southerners had no notion of "repelling them."
They found them convenient.

Lincoln goes even further. He understands that
there is "a proposed amendment to the constitution
to the effect that the federal government shall never
interfere" with slavery in the states where it exists.
Lincoln says *"interfere with the domestic institutions of the States including that of persons held to
service."* Why not say, slavery? His words have
grown as evasive and guilty as those of the constitution itself. He holds that such a provision is now
"implied constitutional law." He adds that he has
"no objection to its being made express and irrevo-
cable." One cannot but linger over the reach and
scope of these words. They mean slavery *forever,*
as far as law and government and the force of arms
can make it. Where now is ultimate extinction?

Lincoln reiterates at the end the assertion of his

February speeches, his passion for peace, his vain attempt to blind himself to the truth. "In your hands, my discontented fellow-citizens," so run the memorable words, "I leave the momentous issue of civil war. The government will not assail you."

Of all the address, the part most admired and quoted is the close. But this is not Lincoln's. The ending as he drafted it was ungraceful and abrupt. Seward suggested the need of ending with "some words of affection—some of calm and cheerful confidence." Seward then wrote a paragraph embodying the beautiful metaphor that gives the close of the speech its remembered charm. Lincoln altered this, rewriting the thought enough to claim it with some conscience as his own. It is a part of the myth that surrounds Lincoln that Seward wrote a sort of rude draft and Lincoln turned it into something real. As one of America's leading historians has put it, "He transmuted Seward's suggestion into pure gold." "The closing passage, of exquisite grace and tenderness," says the historian Schouler, "was roughly sketched by Seward."

But any one with any feeling for the art of letters can judge for himself. Lincoln merely wrote a *variant,* of a beautiful thought, beautifully expressed. But the merit lies in the original thought.

Here stand the two versions. Let the reader judge which is which. The merit of authorship lies with whoever wrote either of them first.

One reads:

"I close. We are not, we must not be alien or enemies but fellow-countrymen and brethren. Although passion has strained our bonds of affection too hardly, they must not, I am sure they will not be broken. The mystic chords which, proceeding from so many battlefields and so many patriot graves, pass through all the hearts and all hearths in this broad continent of ours, will yet again harmonize in their ancient music when breathed upon by the guardian angel of the nation."

The other version reads:—

"I am loath to close. We are not enemies but friends. We must not be enemies. Though passion may have strained, it must not break our bonds of affection. The mystic chords of memory stretching from every battlefield and patriot grave to every hearthstone, all over this broad land will yet swell the chorus of the Union, when touched, as surely they will be, by the better angels of our nature."

At the time when Lincoln made his address the Southern States were busily organizing and arming, taking over property and docks and arsenals and means of war. What Lincoln practically said in his inaugural address was that for the present he proposed to do nothing about it. That was what he proceeded to do.

VI

WAR

WITH the inauguration of Lincoln began the long months of hesitation, of indecision and of inaction which marked the opening of his presidency of the United States. Lincoln had tried in vain to think that there would be no war. In his hesitating and uncertain speeches on his inaugural journey he had in vain "ingeminated peace" where no peace was.

As a matter of fact, from the moment when South Carolina went out, it was absolutely certain that the only alternatives were war or separation. It would indeed have been possible to follow the counsel expressed by old General Scott, and say, "Wayward sisters, depart in peace." In this case the Southerners would have seceded, gladly, without war. They had no wish or thought of conquering or annexing the North. All they wanted was to be done with the North forever.

But to imagine that the seceded South would come back into the Union,—even with a guarantee of state slavery,—by anything else than the force of arms, was mere self-deception. This was Lincoln's great delusion. He either would not or could not see it: the thought of the approaching conflict ap-

palled his soul. In him was none of the fierce hatred
that makes and welcomes war. To him literally, and
without lip-service, all men were and remained
brothers. But this very thought unfitted him for
action. All that could have been done was to make
the coming conflict as small as possible and as
short as possible. Lincoln's unhappy policy made
it as wide as possible and as long as possible. "In
your hands my discontented fellow-countrymen I
leave the momentous issue of civil war." And while
he was thus leaving it, the South found means to
arm and equip and organize, to encourage the hesi-
tant, to combat the unwilling, and to trample under-
foot the remaining forces of union sentiment. They
had, at the South, no illusions as to what was coming.
"Give but little credit to the rumors of an amicable
adjustment," wrote the Confederate Secretary of
War (March 15, 1861) to General Beauregard;
"do not slacken for a moment your energies."
When the war came the Confederacy embraced
virtually every State that we could expect to find
in it.

If Lincoln's policy was, as so many writers have
tried to claim, shrewdly directed at limiting the scope
of the war, it failed. Nothing could have made the
war bigger. If it was aimed at conciliating foreign
opinion, it failed again. Europe took Lincoln at
his word when he said that the war was not over
slavery but over the Union,—in other words, to force
union upon a courageous people overwhelmingly
united against it.

The truth is that Lincoln was lost. From the inauguration till the bombardment of Fort Sumter,

he was carried along, drifting. For the task before him he lacked knowledge and experience and the consciousness of power. Of the conduct of war he knew nothing. As the months went by he learned it,—slowly and ploddingly and certainly, as he had learned to cipher by the firelight in the log-cabin. "He groped his way to the correct method," says the great historian James Rhodes. But for the moment it was beyond him. He must leave it to McClellan.

Of national finance Lincoln was entirely ignorant. He had no experience of such things: and this it was too late to learn. He never tried to learn it. He left it to Salmon Chase. "Lincoln," says the same authority, "was not an adept in finance and left this department to the treasury."

Nor did Lincoln know anything of foreign affairs, of foreign relations and diplomacy. His restricted environment had shut him out from it. His simple and honest disposition made such things distasteful. Nor did he know anything of history, past or current. Once he borrowed a book to read up the Revolutionary War in order to soften the hearts of a country jury with the sufferings of Valley Forge. He had—as an asset later on—the broad common sense and intelligence which is the basis even of diplomatic intercourse. That counted for something even at the start. When Seward (April 1, 1861) proposed a foreign war with half of Europe as a substitute for civil war with half the United States, Lincoln saw the folly of this proposition and laid it gently aside. But for the moment Seward took over all the foreign world and left Lincoln out of it. Of naval affairs Lincoln naturally knew nothing.

It is to be deplored that the myth which has grown up around Lincoln's memory should obscure these obvious truths. For the truth, as has been said and reiterated above, is greater than the myth. What happened in the end was the triumph of Lincoln's spirit over the forces disrupting America. It was Lincoln's soul, his outlook, that conquered,—not his intelligence, nor his policy;—and, least of all, his policy at the opening of the war. The praise and the panegyric which grew around Lincoln after his victory and his assassination were perhaps made all the more extreme from the remembered contrast of the obloquy, the scorn and the distrust which accompanied his initial efforts. His opening presidency was met with the jeers of the South ("the Illinois Ape"), the half-concealed contempt of intellectual New England ("a simple Susan," said the *Springfield Republican*): and by the doubt and distrust of those about him. Edwin Etanton, who was to be, after January 11, 1862, his Secretary of War, and who was to break the silence at Lincoln's deathbed with the words, "Now he belongs to the ages,"—wrote in the summer of 1861 of "the painful imbecility of Lincoln."

The opening month of the new presidency brought with it, in more acute form, the difficulty of what to do about Fort Sumter, where Major Robert Anderson still flew the United States flag, to the rage of South Carolina. Buchanan had left the situation alone. But that could not last. Anderson and his men needed food. They must be fed, or surrender, or starve. In this dilemma sat Lincoln, hopeless,—now thinking this, now that, and doing nothing. He consulted all his Cabinet (March 15, 1861) for long written opinions of alternate courses, fit for an Illinois courtroom. There were men about him, courageous and unhesitating men, such as Captain Gustavus Fox of the United States Navy, who would have settled the question in Jacksonian fashion without a day's delay: steam up, and the United States ships off to provision, and even to arm —why not?—a fort that flew the United States flag.

Would such a course have "lost the allegiance of the South"? It was lost anyway.

The trouble was that Lincoln did not realize that he was President of the United States. There he stood, with behind him the prestige of the greatest republic in the world, with the prestige of the seventy years that linked Washington's name to his own,— with a constituted authority that none could dispute, unless to disrupt and dismember the country. Those on his side must follow him or fall. He had but to stamp on the ground to call forth an army. Later when his hesitating foot fell, the army came,— and after that the shouting millions calling allegiance to "Father Abraham." But that time had not yet come. Lincoln still seemed to think that he must rule by persuading, conciliating and compromising as they did in Illinois politics: that he must consult this interest and avoid alienating that,—all the mechanism of candidacy in place of the autocracy of office. Later, it was all changed. Lincoln ruled. But in the springtime of 1861 he didn't even try to.

His presidential experience opened ill. There was his nightmare journey to Washington, concealed incognito behind the curtains of a sleeper, to avoid an assassin's knife. Then came the inauguration, with sharpshooters on the roofs, then the beleaguered city which almost seemed like an outpost, as it were, in Southern territory, with no adequate defense; in danger,—and still more so after Sumter fell and Virginia was in arms,—of being overwhelmed and its government eclipsed before the regiments from the North could bring it help.

Hay has told us of Lincoln's agonized hours. To those about him he kept a brave face. Personal fear he never knew. "But once," writes his secretary, "after walking the floor alone in silent thought for nearly half an hour, he stopped and gazed long and wistfully out of the window down the Potomac in the direction of the expected ships: and unconscious of other presence in the room, at length broke out in irrepressible anguish in the repeated exclamation, 'Why don't they come! Why don't they come!' "

This was towards the end of April. Between the inauguration and the landing of the Seventh New York from the sea, there had been six long weeks without a plan or policy. A large part of Lincoln's available time was spent, then and long afterwards, in dealing with the importunate mass of office seekers, great and small, and local politicians clamoring for rewards. "The grounds, halls, stairways and closets of the White House," said Seward, "were filled with office seekers." "They stepped in," writes Herndon, "through the half-opened doors of the Executive Mansion: they dogged his steps if he walked: they edged their way through the crowds and thrust their papers in his hands when he rode, and taking it all in all, they well-nigh worried him to death."

Lincoln himself said, "I seem to be like one sitting in a palace assigning apartments to importunate applicants while the structure is on fire and likely soon to perish in ashes."

But this was Lincoln's own fault. There was no greatness in this. Local politicians in rural communities seeking for office must see every one. Rulers of a nation engaged in a struggle of life and death, need see nobody. But Lincoln acted according to his lights. As far as he could, he kept the door open. As far as was possible he saw and talked to them all, and told them stories and little parables, as in New Salem and Springfield. In this, apart from its human tolerance and kindliness, there is little to admire; at least not in such a moment.

A tradition has grown up to the effect that Lincoln told his little stories and his jokes, and read out little "pieces" from Artemus Ward, and the bygone humorist Orpheus C. Kerr (Office-Seeker), because this eased his mind. Thus alone could the great brain find rest, and the harrowed soul a momentary relief. This is nonsense. Lincoln told little stories and jokes because he was Lincoln. He would have told them in Hades.

Meantime the nation, or rather, the North, drifted. While the politicians at Washington, so it has been written, "were vacillating between compromise and resistance, in the South there had been one steady uninterrupted progress towards secession and war." "When I left Washington on Saturday (March 23, 1861)," thus wrote John Dix. "I do not think the administration had any settled policy. It was merely drifting with the current."

General Dix's words were amply corroborated by those of Lincoln's cabinet. Chase, the Secretary of the Treasury, said that the President had "merely the general notion of drifting, the Micawber policy of waiting for something to turn up." Seward himself had already (April 1, 1861) sent to Lincoln the well-known memorandum, entitled *Some Thoughts for the President's Consideration*. In this he said, "We are at the end of a month's administration, and yet without a policy either domestic or foreign." Even Lincoln himself said, as if in defense and explanation of his position, "This government is without a policy."

The view here presented of Lincoln's opening presidency does not represent the sentiments generally expressed and the interpretation placed on the facts by most recognized authorities. Quite the contrary. "It is difficult to see," writes Dr. Rhodes, whose claim as a historian is unsurpassed, "how Lincoln could have bettered the policy to which he gave the keynote in his inaugural address." What is said above, to put it boldly and flatly, is that it is difficult to see how he could have made it worse.

Nor is it possible to challenge and to traverse these opposing statements without a wilderness of references and of documents utterly beyond the compass of this work. For that one must consult the official volumes of the *War Records*, the *Letters and*

Speeches of Abraham Lincoln, and much else. The judgments here expressed are only written for those who have traversed the same ground and who have reached the same conclusion. Such persons while repudiating the absurdities of the Lincoln myth, may still see in Abraham Lincoln one of the most sublime characters in human history.

Even drifting objects must hit something sooner or later. The government of the United States hit Fort Sumter. Lincoln undertook to do what he called "send bread to Anderson." The ill-contrived expedition of relief let loose the bombardment of the fort, and with it the Civil War.

It is no part of the present narrative to relate the course of the American civil war. It remains as one of the great epics of history. It was the last great conflict in which man fought against man. In later wars man fought beside machinery; and now the machine fights the machine. Death mocks mankind. No great struggle was more illuminated by the heroism and devotion of the combatants. No great struggle was ever less degraded by atrocities, cruelty and needless infliction of suffering. Such things as Fort Pillow and the Andersonville stockade were the rare exceptions to the general rule. The devastations of Sherman's march to the sea, though they hit property hard, were not like the smoking farmsteads and the concentration camps of the Boer War. Both sides believed in their cause, the Southerners from first to last, the Northerners more and more as time went on and showed the conflict as one of freedom against slavery. The Southerners saw it otherwise. They had no guilty conscience on the slave question. Nine out of ten honestly believed in the slavery of the negroes as the best and happiest ordinance of society. With this belief they fought as men fight for their own soil and their own homes. For them too, freedom was at stake. Had the issue been anything else but slavery who could question their right? Who could impose by force of arms on a people who would have none of it, a "free union" with their conquerors. But slavery was the key of it all.

This Lincoln began to realize. More and more it was borne in upon his mind that all question of "saving the Union even with slavery" (his reiterated utterance even till August 1862) was mere delusion. In this dawning light he shaped his growing policy.

Lincoln's call for 75,000 militia after the fall of Sumter was followed by a premature invasion of Virginia. Then, as in 1914, few people grasped the long reality of war, grinding slowly towards the end. There followed the battle of Bull Run. It was bravely and fiercely fought. But the ignominious flight by horses and buggies of a rabble of spectators and news-editors, making time for Washington, gave it a grotesque element. Aristocratic Europe jeered over "American battles,"—as inferior as other American products. But the world was soon to see.

In the same summer came random campaigning in Missouri and on the borders and the revolt from its parent state of West Virginia,—a country of mountaineers and villagers with but few slaves. Here General George McClellan, the young hero of the Mexican War, rose as a pocket Napoleon. There followed his elevation to command and the long months of training and organizing that seemed to get nowhere. McClellan's part in the Civil War is still a subject of earnest debate to soldiers and strategists. Civilians settle the matter easily enough.

Lincoln, who could as yet know nothing of how much training and organizing can be sacrificed for the sake of finding the enemy untrained, gave McClellan at this early stage unbounded trust and support. "Don't let them hurry me, is all I ask," said McClellan. (This was Oct. 10, 1861.) "You shall have your own way, I assure you," said Lincoln. A few days later he added, "You must not fight until you are ready." McClellan had no intention of doing that. On November 1 he succeeded General Scott in command of the army and with that he settled down for a winter of real training. Meantime the war on the frontiers gathered and spread like a flame in autumn grass.

With the rise and spread of the conflict in arms rose and spread the question, what now of slavery? It was plain that the question could not be kept out. More and more it appeared as the spearhead of the issue. The North at first had expected easily to overrun the South. With that they feared an insurrection of the downtrodden negroes against their masters. Generals, such as Benjamin Butler at Annapolis, offered the help of Northern arms if needed. The South contemptuously refused. The fear was idle. The negroes never rose: never thought of it. They went on serving their "masters." They even served against themselves, so to speak, as body servants and such in the war. There was no more danger of an uprising of the slaves on the plantations than of the girls of the Massachusetts factories who worked, in the days of "Uncle Tom's Cabin," twelve hours a day and at times fourteen.

CONTRABANDS COMING INTO THE UNION LINES
(*A contemporary drawing by Thomas Nast in* HARPER'S WEEKLY, *1863*)

Both classes were to "rise" later on. But this was still noon-day in the nineteenth century. Color and labor both knew their place.

There was no rising. But other slave problems arose. The Confederate general, John B. Magruder, facing Butler at Fort Montroe, used negro slaves to dig on earthworks. When some of them escaped to Butler's lines, he dealt with them as "contraband of war," and refused to return them to a "foreign state." Whenever the Northern forces broke into Southern territory and dispossessed the owners, the negroes flocked to the Northern camps, harmless and inquisitive as children. Some generals like Halleck in Missouri and Sherman in Kentucky and Dix, of the American flag, refused to follow Butler's lead. They sent the negroes away. "We have nothing to do with slaves," said Dix, "we are neither negro stealers, nor negro catchers." Others thought the contrary. General Frémont, the pathfinder, fighting to clear rebellion from Missouri, declared martial law in the state, with death for those in arms, and freedom for all the slaves of rebels.

But this was going too far. Frémont's proclamation covered much more than the war-status of the slaves. It would have turned every Confederate soldier into a criminal, every sailor to a pirate and the war to an indiscriminate massacre. "Rebels" or not, the Confederates were in fact belligerents and were treated as such. Yet, oddly enough, people in the Northern States childishly resented the actions of England and France in doing in form what they did themselves in fact;—the recognition of "belligerency."

Frémont, however, had substituted words for deeds. Beaten in the field he almost lost all federal control of Missouri. Lincoln countermanded his orders and "let him go."

Apart from Frémont's sweeping proclamation, no very definite action was taken in regard to slavery in the first summer and autumn of the war (1861). The Republican majority in Congress were inclined to follow Lincoln's lead in hitting slavery where they could. They answered General McGruder's action in using slave labor for war purposes by an act (Aug. 6, 1861), declaring the freedom of all slaves thus used.

But the position of parties and public opinion was still confused. The out-and-out abolitionists had faced about in a new direction. They wanted to let the South go. Wendell Phillips, speaking in Boston against the war, was shouted down. Garrison declared that to "think of whipping the South into subjection and extorting allegiance from millions of people at the cannon's mouth is utterly chimerical." Many still thought, or tried to think, that the war would pass and the conflict somehow be composed. Others saw more clearly. The aged historian George Bancroft, never a Republican, writing to Lincoln (Nov. 15, 1861), said, "Your administration has fallen upon times which will be remembered as long as human events find a record. . . . Civil war is the instrument of Divine Providence to root out social slavery. Posterity will not be satisfied with the result unless the consequences of the war shall effect an increase of free states. This is the universal expectation and hope of men of all parties."

Bancroft's language is a little cryptic. Does he mean "States of the Union" or "states of the World"? Lincoln realized the gravity of either meaning and how closely it coincided with his own thought. But he answered cautiously, "The main thought of the closing paragraph of your letter is one which does not escape my attention, and with which I must deal

with all due caution, and with the best judgment
I can bring to it."

For already Lincoln had in the front of his mind
the plan for a first step towards "ultimate extinction." This was the abolition of slavery by "buying
it out," compensated abolition, such as England had
used for colonial slavery in 1833. In the very month
of Bancroft's letter, he had drafted a bill for buying
out the slaves of Delaware. The plan was moderate
enough: All persons born after the adoption of the
act to be free: all slaves over thirty-five, or reaching
that age in future, to be bought into freedom by
the federal government and all slaves forever free
after the year 1893. Lincoln had been calculating
that the whole cost of it was less than the cost of
the war to the North for half a day! This was the
beginning of abolition by purchase, much talked of
for years, before and after the Proclamation of Emancipation. Apart from the District of Columbia,
it was never actually adopted.

To Lincoln's perplexities was added during that
autumn (1861) the episode known as the *Trent*
affair. An American naval captain stopped a British
mail steamer on the high seas and took out of it,
by a display of force and against protest, two envoys
from the Confederacy, officially accredited to England and to France. The Northern States rang with
jubilant applause, shared and voiced officially by the
Secretary of the Navy and by Congress. There was
no Atlantic cable to tone it down with warning; to
tell America that all England echoed with indignation,—some of it real, some hysterical and some of
it worked up for the purpose; and to remind America

of the overwhelming power of the British navy, and of the arrogance that might go with overwhelming power even in a decent people.

Now there was at this time a vast international fiction called international law. It had grown up out of the set of rules that regulated gentlemanly fighting in the Middle Ages,—just as school fighting condemns kicking in the stomach or hitting below the belt. In the seventeenth, eighteenth and nineteenth centuries it had grown to larger proportions: for it had been increased by the content of various general treaties,—bilateral and multilateral. In this guise it professed to regulate the conduct of war, and especially the status of neutrals, and transport over the sea in war-time. The recent Great War has crumbled it all into débris. Henceforth there are no rules for the conduct of war except those imposed by the humanity of the combatants themselves, or dictated by their apprehensions. But at this time the superior power of the great nations still preferred to operate under the supposed sanction of a higher law.

Under international law the British had always claimed wide rights of searching neutral ships, and if need be, confiscating ships, and cargoes and passengers. There being no submarines all this was done with the decent corroboration of a prize court. The Americans had always protested against the extent and width of the British claim.

Now, in the *Trent* affair, the rôles were reversed. England argued against the right of capture and the Americans in favor of it. Lord Palmerston admitted (privately) that the British were wrong. But the British legal authorities found a way to square the decisions of the past and the claims of the present by saying that the American Captain Wilkes was "wrong" because he *hadn't seized enough*. If he had taken the ship also, as well as the envoys, he would have been "right." This comic decision was called international law, without a laugh.

But Lincoln's common sense showed him the fallacy of it all. It was just a case of superior force, and nothing else. The envoys were just "white elephants" on his hands. He and Seward had to give them up and they gave them up. British troopships were landing regiments in British North America, as an evidence of the force of international law.

The whole current of the episode injured the relations of the North with England. The governing class, the aristocracy and the interests of commerce were, for the moment, overwhelmingly for the South. Nor can we blame too much the failure of England to rally to the cause of "freedom." Apart from Frémont and the abolitionists, and the rising murmur of many voices not yet heard across the ocean, there was no thought of that.

With the opening of the new year (1862) the thunder of the war broke in earnest and its operations assumed a scale that made the previous conflicts look like a mere skirmish.

The storm broke first in the west. Ulysses S. Grant, whose name was now first heard by the outer world, operating in Kentucky, moved rapidly on Forts Henry and Donelson, that guarded the Cumberland and the Tennessee rivers. He took them, as it were, in a single blow, the first of his sledge hammer strokes of the war, with "unconditional surrender" (Feb. 16, 1862) for the defenders. Lincoln, still painfully occupied with his opening studies in strategy, got from Grant a first lesson in the art of war: and did not forget it.

Grant's victory opened a pathway southward into the Confederacy. Within two months the Confederacy was fighting for its life in the great battle of Shiloh,—in the very south of Tennessee. "Had the Grant of Shiloh been the Grant of Donelson" (a gentle way in which Mr. Rhodes indicates certain well-known facts), Shiloh would have anticipated Vicksburg. Lincoln was urged, after Shiloh, to get rid of Grant. His well-known answer, "I can't spare this man: he fights," shows his growing knowledge and confidence. It is typical of his achievement.

The blow from the northern direction was followed by a still harder one against the Confederacy from the southern side. The navy, under Admiral Farragut, smashed its way past the barriers, booms and defenses of the Mississippi. New Orleans fell to the North (April 28, 1862), never to be retaken. The capture brought with it the control of a city of 168,000 people by Benjamin Butler and his Union force of 2,500 soldiers. Incidentally it put Butler in charge of a negro population of some eighty thousand souls, newly acquired. Butler's stern but effective martial law, his civic order and his conquest of yellow fever are commonplaces of history; so, too, his personal crookedness and his famous "woman order" which caused Jefferson Davis to proclaim him "an outlaw and a common enemy of mankind, . . . to be immediately executed by hanging." He died in bed in 1893.

Butler did not, as accused, enlist the slaves against their masters. He did enlist free negroes: but the Southerners had already done that too. Nor was there need now for General Butler to deal with the negro question—in the summer of 1862—with subtleties of the "contraband" order. The times had moved on. Congress itself and the President as commander-in-chief were altering with every month the war status of the negro. Short of declaring free the slaves of peaceful persons in Louisiana, Butler could go as far as he liked.

Others had already gone further. On the southern coast some 10,000 negroes were already free men under Northern government.

The capture of Port Royal in South Carolina (Nov. 7, 1861) had thrown into Federal hands coast on both sides of the Savannah River, seventy miles in all. This was the sea island cotton country, rich in produce, and black as ink with slaves. The white masters fled, burning what they could. The slaves, frightened at first by bogey stories of Yankee cruelty, came crawling back. When the spring opened General Sherman had a negro population of nearly 10,000 to look after. They were fed, organized, set to work and given wages. Then came General David Hunter, Lincoln's own friend, an anti-slavery man and warm to the heart in the cause. "Slavery and martial law in a free country," proclaimed Hunter (May 1862), "are altogether incompatible. The persons in these three states, Georgia, Florida and South Carolina heretofore held as slaves are therefore declared forever free." But this again was going too fast and too far. Hunter, like Frémont, was using words for things beyond his power. Yet Lincoln's countermanding proclamation (May 19, 1862) struck a new note. He must reserve for himself alone, he said, the question whether as "commander-in-chief of the army and navy it was competent for him to declare the slaves of any State free" and "whether it shall have become a necessity indispensable to the maintenance of government to exercise such a supposed power." This clearly indicates what was in his mind.

Meantime Congress was taking action far beyond that of 1861. Nor could they avoid it. "During the long session from Dec. 2, 1861, to July 17, 1862," says John Hay, "the subject (of slavery) seemed to touch every topic at some point." An act of March 13 prohibited officers of the army from using military forces to return run-away slaves. This turned the previous incidental humanity of odd leaders into the military duty of all. An act of July 19, 1862, turned into Federal law the original platform of the Republican party by declaring free all persons within the territories of the United States. Most notable of all was the Confiscation Act, a statute significantly entitled, "An act to destroy slavery under the powers of War" (July 17, 1862). This went far beyond the act of August 6 of the preceding year. It referred nominally only to the slaves of rebels but this meant virtually all the slaves in the rebel states. It set free any of them who escaped into army lines, or were captured, or deserted, into the control of the United States. A further provision authorized the President "to employ as many persons of African descent as he may deem necessary and proper for the suppression of the rebellion," and to "organize and use them in such ways as he may judge best." By interpretation this meant the enlisting of negro regiments, which began forthwith.

Most pressing of all was the question of the slaves in the border states. This Lincoln had close at heart. For the old conception that a slave was property died hard everywhere. And in any case it seemed unfair that a particular group or class should bear all the financial cost of a rise in national morality. The owners of the border State slaves must be considered; especially as they might still go over to the South.

There were that year in Delaware 1,789 slaves, in Maryland 87,188, in Kentucky 225,400, in Missouri 114,965; and in the District of Columbia, under the Federal government itself, were 3,181. Lincoln "figured" that the whole lot of them could be bought out for about $173,000,000 ($400 apiece) which was less than three months' cost of the war.

On the 6th of March the President sent a message to Congress to the effect that "the United States ought to coöperate with any State which may adopt gradual abolition of slavery, giving to such State pecuniary aid." The message was widely circulated in the press, which gave Lincoln the opportunity to supplement it with a communication to the New York *Times*. "Eighty-seven days' cost of this war," he wrote, "would pay for all the slaves in Delaware,

Maryland, District of Columbia, Kentucky and Missouri. Do you doubt that it would shorten the war more than eighty-seven days?"

He called a conference at the White House (March 10, 1862) of all the members of Congress from the border States and laid the plan before them. He asked for no answer, only for consideration. It is doubtful if his own mind was fully made up. He still "disclaimed any intent to injure the interests or wound the susceptibilities of the slave States." This still looks like the vanishing dream of retaining the Union with slavery.

But for the District of Columbia, where the slaves were an eyesore to mankind and a reproach to freedom, Lincoln did not need to wait. At his suggestion Congress passed an act (April 11, 1862) setting the District slaves free with a compensation of three hundred dollars per slave to any owners not in rebellion. This, as it turned out, was the only money paid in the United States for compensated abolition.

As if to accentuate the gravity of the moment, louder still rose the thunder of the war,—louder and more ominous. McClellan moved at last. His trained and organized army moved majestically by sea down the Potomac. There followed the ghastly record and the terrible slaughter of the peninsular campaign of 1862. McClellan with 100,000 men sat down in front of Yorktown,—"afraid," wrote Hay to Nicolay, "either to fight or run." "No one but McClellan," wrote the Confederate Joseph E. Johnston, "would have hesitated to attack." Lincoln now turning to a strategist, tried in vain to prod him on. Within a few miles of Richmond with overwhelming forces, McClellan hesitated and delayed till the gathered armies of the South, inferior, but led by Lee and Jackson, fought his army to the verge of destruction. "Lee and Jackson," writes Colonel Henderson, "did more for the Confederacy than 200,000 soldiers for the Union." McClellan, we are told "made a masterly retreat." Lincoln, wanting more than that, removed him from command. General Pope, coming from the West with a mouthful of braggart phrases, took over the remains of the army and led it to destruction at (second) Bull Run (Aug. 29, 30, 1862). This was the Nadir of Union fortunes, the army in retreat, a Southern army gathering to invade the North, and Washington again in imminent danger.

VII

EMANCIPATION

FOR Lincoln the crisis had come. Something must be done to animate the spirit of the North. "Things had gone from bad to worse," he said afterwards, "until I felt that we had reached the end of our rope on the plan of operations we had been pursuing." And he knew what he meant to do, to alter the spirit of the conflict. "It has got to be," he said.

For Lincoln stood now on his own feet. He needed no briefs of advice from his cabinet. "I expect to maintain this contest until successful," so he wrote down his resolve in the dark days of McClellan's failure, "or till I die, or am conquered, or my term expires, or Congress or the country forsakes me."

All about him as the national danger grew was a tumult of voices shouting about slavery—urging, protesting. Not only the abolitionists and the extremists but thousands of people of all ranks clamored that the time had come to declare slavery at an end. But a tumult of other voices answered back, protesting against "interference by the general government" with a "local domestic question appertaining to the States." The words are those of Secretary

149

Welles and reflect the sentiment of the cabinet. Even such a patriot and such a fighter as Governor Andrew of Massachusetts had just said (May 14, 1862) that the war was "the struggle of the people to vindicate their own rights, to retain and invigorate the institutions of their fathers." There was protest, too, against any disregard of the border States. The difficulty there was peculiar. The more loyal the slaveholders were, the better seemed their right to keep their slaves.

All of this, Lincoln heard and did not hear. That summer he walked alone,—or, if we may believe his own reverent assertion,—took counsel with "his Maker." If a man must stand alone, above and beyond human guidance, facing a supreme responsibility and turns for help to a Supreme Being in whose existence he had come earnestly to believe he may be said to "walk with God." So walked Abraham Lincoln. By the time midsummer had come, Lincoln's mind, thus guided, as he felt, was made up. He would set the slaves free,—as far as lay in his power, as President of the United States and as commander-in-chief of its armies. For the rest he would trust to that higher power to which more and more his mind had turned.

But one difficulty still remained,—the slavery in the border States. Lincoln,—so he himself felt,—had neither the constitutional power nor the military and physical power to set free the slaves in the border States. He could only appeal to those who had it, and appeal through Congress to their fellow citizens to aid them to bear the economic loss involved. For Lincoln could not as a war measure declare free the slaves in the rebel States without at least giving the border States a chance to act. Otherwise he foresaw that there might happen exactly what did happen; the owners in the border States might lose their slaves for nothing,—as they ultimately did.

On the 12th of July, 1862, Lincoln again called a conference of representatives of the border States. He could not tell them what was in his mind,—that he intended as commander-in-chief to proclaim the freedom of slaves in the rebel States. But he urged, he begged, he implored them, to join with the national government in a plan of compensated abolition.

"In my opinion," he said, "if you had all voted for the resolution in the gradual emancipation message of last March, the war would now be substantially ended. . . . You are patriots and statesmen . . . I pray you to consider this proposition. . . . Our common country is in great peril. . . . To you, more than to any other the privilege is given to assure its happiness."

The slaveholders heard him and went away and like Pharaoh they hardened their hearts. Greed miscalculated its own gains. Gradual abolition bills were brought in, considered, revised, shelved and in the end perished. The slaveholders could not believe that slavery was really at an end.

Nor can we blame too much their want of foresight. Even at this time and later, Lincoln still used language that implied that slavery *might* remain as an institution of part of the republic.

We have as evidence his famous public letter of

August 22, 1862, addressed to Horace Greeley. In those days newspaper editors were tribunes of the people, not employees of the proprietor. This arose from the value placed on the personal expression of opinion rather than the impersonal value of news. Such was Horace Greeley, the tribune of the New York *Tribune*. He had made in his paper an appeal to Lincoln, entitled *"The Prayer of Twenty Million People."* He urged that there was nothing but futility in "attempts to put down the rebellion and at the same time uphold its inciting cause."

Lincoln published an open reply,—one of his most famous pronouncements. "If there be those who would not save the Union unless they could at the same time destroy slavery, I do not agree with them. My paramount object in this struggle is to save the Union, and it is not either to save or to destroy slavery. If I could save the Union without freeing any slave, I would do it: and if I could save it by freeing some and leaving others alone, I would also do that."

It seems a pity that Lincoln could not add to this communication that in his opinion it was no longer possible to save the Union with slavery. But that he was keeping to himself. He had already drafted (July 22) the proclamation that was to smite slavery to the ground. He was only waiting to give it to the world.

For when Lincoln wrote to Greeley the long anguish of his indecision was all over. He knew what he meant to do. He could not save the Union with slavery: he was going to save it without.

We know that all this was in Lincoln's mind when he talked (on July 12) with the men of the border States. For it was on the next day that he first gave utterance to what he meant to do. The solemnity of the occasion fitted his mood and thought: for he rode in a carriage with Secretary Welles and Secretary Seward to the funeral of a little child,—the infant son of their colleague Edwin Stanton. And here Lincoln spoke, so Welles tells us, earnestly and gravely of the situation: told them that he had "almost come to the conclusion" that he must free the slaves by proclamation: and told them further that "this was the first occasion when he had mentioned the subject to any one." Neither Welles nor Seward had suspected that this was in Lincoln's mind. They could not comment or advise. It seemed to Welles "a new departure for the President."

A few days later (July 22, 1862) the cabinet were called together to be told of the President's determination. We know of what happened from a memorandum afterwards set down by Carpenter (the artist who painted the historic picture of the Signing of the Proclamation) as the words told him by Abraham Lincoln.

"I now determined upon the adoption of the Emancipation policy: and without consultation with, or the knowledge of, the cabinet, I prepared the original draft of the proclamation and after anxious thought called a cabinet meeting upon the subject. I said to the cabinet that I had resolved upon the step and had not called them together to ask their advice, but to lay the subject matter of the proclamation before them, suggestions as to which would be in order after they had read it."

With that Lincoln read out the draft of a proclamation, the subject of which was to declare his intentions of a further recommendation of compensated abolition of slavery for States not in rebellion, and his order, as Commander-in-chief, that all slaves in any States still in rebellion on January 1, 1863, should "then thenceforth and forever be free."

When Lincoln had finished, Edwin Stanton and the attorney-general expressed approval without qualification; Salmon Chase, approval with a qualification. "I said that I should give such a measure my cordial support but I should prefer that no new expression on the subject of compensation should be made: and I thought that the measure of emancipation could be much better and more quietly accomplished by allowing generals to organize and arm the slaves, thus avoiding depredation and massacre on the one hand, and support to the insurrection on the other, and by directing the commanders of departments to proclaim emancipation within their districts as soon as practicable. But I regarded this as so much better than inaction on the subject, that I should give it my entire support."

Montgomery Blair dissented. He said that the proclamation would "cost the administration the fall elections." To a politician this was worse than slavery.

Seward as usual hit the nail on the head. Emancipation was just and right, but this—the dark hour of ill-fortune—was the wrong moment.

"It might be viewed as the last measure of an exhausted government, a cry for help; the government stretching forth its hands to Ethiopia, instead of Ethiopia stretching forth her hands to the government."

Lincoln's common sense saw the wisdom of this.

LINCOLN'S FIRST READING OF THE PROCLAMATION
TO HIS CABINET

(From a contemporary engraving)

He put the Proclamation in his desk, and continued his solitary communing and his prayers for victory.

Victory, or something like it, came. McClellan, by a counsel of despair, was restored to command. There seemed to be no one else. Lincoln disregarded the objections of his cabinet. The South prepared to "drive the invader from the soil" (Davis to General Lee) and to turn the tables by an invasion of the North. Lee carried his army across the Potomac into Maryland. He staked everything on McClellan's ineptitude. Lee's 50,000 men had but little food, thousands of them had no shoes: they were short of equipment and of transport. McClellan had everything. Lee, as if contemptuous of McClellan, had even temporarily divided his advancing army in two. By chance, or providence, a copy of Lee's orders for the disposition of his troops fell into McClellan's hands. The ensuing operations culminating in the battle of Antietam (also called Sharpsburg) (Aug. 17, 1862) were a victory for McClellan, or as near to a victory as McClellan could get. Lee's invasion failed. His army moved south again, intact and unmolested. This was the end of McClellan.

But it was the beginning of freedom. Here at least was victory enough on which to base the dictates of the victor. The time for the Proclamation had come.

"The President," so recorded John Hay in his Journal, "wrote the Proclamation on Sunday morning (Sept. 21) carefully. He called the cabinet together on Monday, Sept. 22, made a little talk to them and read the momentous document."

The cabinet met at the White House. All the members were present. "There were some general talk," so records Secretary Chase in his diary, "and the President mentioned that Artemus Ward had sent him his book. He proposed," adds Chase with dry disapproval, "to read a chapter which he thought very funny. He read it and seemed to enjoy it very much: the heads also (except Stanton) of course."

We do not know whether the "of course" refers to the subservience of the heads or to their exuberant sense of humor. Nor do we know why Stanton is an exception,—presumably by his lack of the sense of fun. Yet Stanton read Dickens at this time day and night. When Dickens,—as an aged and weary egotist surfeited with success,—was in Washington six years later he met Stanton and wrote home, "He is famous for his acquaintance with the minutest details of my books. He never went to sleep (during the war time) without first reading something from my books." In this way Stanton's claim to fame and his sense of humor seem both assured. Perhaps poor Artemus Ward was beneath him.

What Abraham Lincoln read was as follows:

HIGH-HANDED OUTRAGE AT UTICA

In the Faul of 1856, I showed my show in Utiky, a trooly grate sitty in the State of New York.

The people gave me a cordyal recepshun. The press was loud in her prases.

1 day as I was givin a descripshun of my Beests and Snaiks in my usual flowry stile what was my skorn & disgust to see a big burly feller walk up to the cage containin my wax figgers of the Lord's Last Supper, and cease Judas Iscarrot by the feet and drag him out on the ground. He then commenced fur to pound him as hard as he cood.

"What under the son are you abowt?" cried I.

Sez he, "What did you bring this pussylanermus cuss here fur?" & hit the wax figger another tremenjis blow on the hed.

Sez I, "You egrejus ass, that air's a wax figger— a representashun of the false 'Postle."

Sez he, "That's all very well fur you to say but I tell you, old man, that Judas Iscarrot can't show hisself in Utiky with impunerty by a darn site!" with which observashun he kaved in Judassis hed. The young man belonged to 1 of the first famerlies in Utiky. I sood him, and the Joory brawt in a verdick of Arson in the 3d degree.

When Lincoln had made an end of Artemus Ward his voice, we are told, took a graver tone.

"Gentlemen," he said, "I have as you are aware thought a great deal about the relation of this war to slavery. . . . Several weeks ago I read you an order I had prepared. . . . Ever since then my mind has been much occupied with this subject. . . . I think the time has come now. When the rebel army was at Frederick, I determined, as soon as it should be driven out of Maryland, to issue a proclamation of emancipation. . . . I said nothing to any one but I made a promise to myself and to my Maker. The rebel army is now driven out and I am going to fulfill that promise. I have got you together to hear what I have written down. I do not wish your advice upon the main matter for that I have determined for myself."

The full text of the Proclamation appears as an appendix to this book. The part essential for the present exposition is found in the words

". . . on the first day of January in the year of our Lord one thousand eight hundred and sixty-three, all persons held as slaves within any State, or designated part of a State, the people whereof shall then be in rebellion against the United States, shall be then, thenceforward and forever free."

"All listened with profound attention to the reading," so relates Gideon Welles, the Secretary of the Navy, "and it was, I believe, assented to by every member."

Seward took the document for attestation to the State Department. The great seal was attached. Lincoln signed it that afternoon. The newspapers published it on the morning of Tuesday, September 23, 1862.

The thing was done. The governors of a number of the eastern States happened to meet in conference at Altoona in Pennsylvania the day after the publication. They had not been summoned because of the Proclamation. Things moved too slowly for that. They had been called to take action against the invasion, which action Antietam had rendered needless. But they gave to emancipation their instant and unqualified support and reiterated their devotion to the cause. Not so the governors of the border States. They withheld their signatures of approval. But Lincoln had with him the firm official support of seventeen loyal States, as against the hesitating of five. When Congress met, Democratic opposition raised its head in vain. In spite of the Democratic gain in the fall elections, the house voted by seventy-eight to fifty-one that "the proclamation of the President is warranted by the constitution and that the policy of emancipation is well adapted to hasten the restoration of peace."

Such too in all the wilderness of discussion, was the general faith and sentiment of the country.

Meantime the fatal months ran out as the year

passed to its close. The thunder of war did not lessen. The attempt to reinvade Virginia moved from disaster to disaster. The year closed with Burnside's hopeless assault of the heights and the stonewalls of Fredericksburg on the Rappahannock. Here a thousand Union men fell in a few minutes facing without cover a sheet of flame. The total Northern casualties were 12,653. Burnside moaned over his dead soldiers like the Roman Augustus over the legions of Quintilius Varus. "Oh, those men over there! I am thinking of them all the time."

This was war indeed. In such a crucible was being forged the new America. This is the very judgment of the Lord of the Second Inaugural address.

Nor did the fierce conflict in the west, where Bragg now invaded Kentucky bring Northern victory any nearer.

Thus closed the old year in storm and thunder. And with the coming of the new, with January 1, 1863, Abraham Lincoln gave forth his final Proclamation of Emancipation.

It followed closely along the lines of the announcement of three months before. Its closing sentence, composed not by Lincoln but by Chase, stands among the sublime things of history:

"And upon this act, sincerely believed to be an act of justice warranted by the constitution upon military necessity, I invoke the considerate judgment of mankind and the gracious favor of Almighty God."

VIII

EPILOGUE

IT is no part of the present work to narrate the
ensuing history of the Civil War from Lincoln's
Proclamation to its close. The titanic struggle
reached its climax in the months following the emancipation of the slaves. In the summer of 1863 came
the great victories of Gettysburg and Vicksburg in
the opening of the month of July. This meant the
repulse of the Confederate invasion of the Northern
States, henceforth never to be renewed, and the
opening of the Mississippi from the Northern States
to the Gulf of Mexico to the gunboats and the commerce of the North. "The father of waters," to use
Lincoln's oft-quoted phrase, "runs unvexed to the
sea." The Confederacy was cut in two; the vast
supplies from Texas no longer available for its use.

As all can see it now, Gettysburg and Vicksburg
were the turning points beyond which the end was
in sight. Not that such a vision was clear at the
time. The South was still solid, compact,—bisected
but nowhere broken. Lee's great army had dragged
itself slowly away uncaptured. With the army of
Virginia safely across the Potomac and reorganized,
the South seemed as impregnable as ever. Whether
Lee escaped by the ineptitude of General Meade, or

by the exhaustion of his soldiers, is a matter for the military historians to discuss forever.

Nor had the Proclamation of January 1st as yet made an immediate and visible difference to the war or to the world. In our present era of shouting radios and flickering shadows, it would have been all over humanity and back in half an hour,—with exchanges rising and falling, statesmen approving, national demonstrations, volunteers and a wilderness of immediate consequence. Not so then.

There was no illumination to herald the announcement of freedom. But the lamps shone brighter in many a humble window, and little groups gathered for prayers of thanksgiving. This new spirit spread. Those who went to the war from the North from now on went with a noble purpose, fighting not alone for American union but for human freedom. For union, if it could be, but never now at the price of slavery. Lincoln's values were reversed.

The spirit spread abroad. The Atlantic cable—laid in Buchanan's time—had only clicked out a few words and stopped. It lay broken on the bed of the Atlantic throughout the Civil War. It needed a month for news to reach England; a month to hear what the English thought of it.

The news overlapped in both directions. There was no continuous "contact," no international thought.

The first reaction of aristocratic England to the proclamation had been that of obloquy and ridicule. The London *Times* called it "the execrable expedient of a servile insurrection," and said that the "attempt to restore the Union is as hopeless as would be here the attempt to restore the Heptarchy." But this could not last. Truth prevails. The light spread. The people of England, the plain people first, realized that the great war in America was a struggle for human freedom and their ridicule was hushed in expectation of its end.

But for Lincoln himself, the issue of the Proclamation made a great change. With the liberation of the slaves, he found his soul. Henceforth his path, if arduous, was clear. Doubt and hesitation were gone. There was now in the President—for such he had truly become—an inflexibility of purpose: no thought of cessation: no dream of compromise: nothing but a fight to the end.

"Fondly do we hope, fervently do we pray, that this mighty scourge of war shall speedily pass away. Yet, if God wills that it continue till all the wealth piled by the bondsman's two hundred and fifty years of unrequited toil shall be sunk, and until every drop of blood drawn with the lash shall be paid by another drawn with the sword, as was said three thousand years ago, still it must be said, 'The judgments of the Lord are true and righteous altogether.'"

With this inflexible determination, Lincoln combined, for all those distressed by the war, for the wounded, for the prisoners, for those under sentence of court-martial, an equally inflexible human kindness that firmly stayed the military hand, and checked the vengeance of the law. Lincoln's pardons are as beautiful as those from Heaven.

With that he governed.

Note the change in the journal and letters of young John Hay. "The Tycoon is in fine whack," he writes, a month after Gettysburg (his language in the letters not aiming at the dignified, even sanctimonious tone of the history, and "Tycoon" being a pet name for his employer). "I have rarely seen him more serene and busy. He is managing this war, the draft, foreign relations, and planning a reconstruction all at once. I never knew with what tyrannous authority he rules the cabinet till now. The most important things he decides and there is no cavil. I am growing more convinced that the country absolutely demands that he should be kept where he is till this thing is over."—Note that Hay had evidently doubted it before—"There is no man in the country so wise, so gentle and so firm."

And a little later (Sept. 11, 1863) Hay writes:—

"Some well-meaning newspapers advise the President to keep his fingers out of the pie, and all that sort of thing. The truth is, if he did, the pie would be a sorry mess. The old man sits here and wields like a backwoods Jupiter the bolts of war and the machinery of government with a hand especially steady and equally firm."

Yet the final victory was still far away.

The war indeed, even after Gettysburg and Vicksburg, as far as numbers and battles went, had little more than begun. There was still to follow the heroic fighting for the possession of Tennessee and with it the power to smash through the western wall of the Confederacy. There was still to come Sherman's famous march to the sea (1864-65) and his grim devastation with fire and sword,—the war against women and children, against hearths and homes, against humanity itself—to which wars have ever since been degraded. Sherman's methods were to be reproduced by General Weyler in Cuba, and in the "methods of barbarism" used in South Africa.

LINCOLN ENTERING RICHMOND, APRIL 3, 1865
(*From a contemporary engraving*)

From these things, not from defeat and death in the field, survive the bitter memories that refuse to die. So it was to be with the South.

More than all, the invasion of Virginia had to be undertaken all over again. Fire and sword must still force a way through forest and scrub and river from the Potomac to Richmond. All the dead who fell under McClellan and Hooker and Burnside must

165

rise again in the new conscripts drawn from the North for a later and greater harvest of death. And in the new leader, General Grant, a grim reaper was found. He won the war in Virginia not by strategy but by brute slaughter. Whether or not this is generalship is again a military question. The most illustrious of Grant's subordinates, General Francis Walker, afterwards denounced his method as the very "negation of generalship." Grant could win by having two of his own men killed for one of Lee's. On the assumption that there was no other and better way to do it, this must have been right.

So in the end the armies closed in on Richmond. The Confederacy was pierced, broken, and compressed on every side—harassed by sea and land—its armies without shelter, without equipment, almost without food, fighting heroically to the end, without a break in the ranks, without a murmur of treason —a wonderful human epic.

And the slaves never rose. When the remnant of Lee's army surrendered at Appomattox, they were standing meekly by. Those who hate the very idea of slavery must in all fairness weigh and measure these facts in their judgments on past history. The slaves never rose during the war and they took no vengeance afterwards. There were no rising and massacrings of their late masters in retaliation for their "wrong." Mostly they didn't know they had any. On the plantations, in lost corners undisturbed by the war, they stayed at work. Where the track of fire and sword had passed they flocked about, muddled and confused among the Freedman's Bureaus and the military régime and the smoking ruins that had replaced the sunny cornfields of the South.

They were lost in the new vacuity of their freedom. And the hand that could have guided them was cold and still.

We know now how Lincoln's soul uprose with joy to this task that he alone beyond all men could best perform. He who never knew hatred could bring peace. He who could not bear dispute could hush argument. He who could not harbor anger might soften it in others. Peace and the Union, and the great wrong of slavery blotted out with tears and atoned in blood; oblivion of the past, the freedom of all men,—his task and he knew it.

It was all so clear in his mind. Lincoln knew what he meant to do. He would forestall the vengeance of the politicians. When it was clear that the end was in sight, he went down the Potomac and talked—in the cabin of the steamer *River Queen*—with Grant and Sherman. The terms they gave at Appomattox and later to General Johnston, so framed as to place military honor to block the path of civil vengeance, were Lincoln's terms. Set thus they made a precedent. There were no trials. Vengeance belonged elsewhere.

There were strange wild scenes in Washington on Monday, the 10th of April, 1865, when it was learned in the city that Lee had surrendered the day before. A survivor, of Lincoln's bodyguard—who lived, as Judge McBride, to be present at its last roll call in 1915—has described the tumult in the streets that

167

followed the announcement. "Men yelled, screamed, shouted, cheered, laughed and wept." A crowd gathered outside the War Department. They shouted for speeches. Secretary Stanton and Montgomery Blair harangued the crowd. Andrew Johnson, the Vice-President, tore the air with shouts for vengeance. "What shall we do," he yelled, "with the leaders of the rebel host? If I were President, I would arrest them as traitors, I would try them as traitors, and, by the Eternal, I would hang them as traitors!"

Then some one shouted, "To the White House," and in a few moments a surging crowd was calling for the President. He came and stood at an upper window and for a time the cheers drowned everything else.

Then Lincoln raised his hand and the crowd was still and he said:

"My friends, you want a speech but I cannot make one at this time. . . . I must take time to think. . . . There is one thing I will do, however. You have a band with you. There is one piece of music I have always liked. For the last few years it has not been popular in the North. But now by virtue of my prerogative as President and Commander-in-Chief of the Army and Navy, I declare it contraband of war and our lawful prize. I ask the band to play Dixie."

"The crowd," says Judge McBride, "went wild, and for probably the first time after the fall of Fort Sumter, the tune of Dixie was greeted with cheers from Union throats."

Thus was Lincoln setting about his task. Four
nights later he was carried unconscious from Ford's
Theatre, the bullet of the assassin in his brain. He
was laid in a little brick house over the way.

All night Lincoln lived, unconscious, at times
moaning, but his breathing firm and regular. His

PRESIDENT LINCOLN'S FUNERAL PROCESSION
(*From* HARPER'S WEEKLY, *May, 1865*)

great frame, his iron strength, his unconscious will
fought against his Maker's decree. It must have
seemed hard to go. Then with the morning the
light came, and he died—on his face, we are told,
"unspeakable peace."

It seems strange that he had to go. It seems at
first as if he were taken away at the very moment

when his service could have been greatest to the world. But perhaps it is otherwise. Lincoln living would have helped to compose the strife of a nation. Lincoln dead helps to save the world.

APPENDIX

FINAL EMANCIPATION PROCLAMATION
(January 1, 1863)

BY THE PRESIDENT OF THE UNITED STATES OF AMERICA:

A Proclamation

Whereas, on the twenty-second day of September, in the year of our Lord one thousand eight hundred and sixty-two, a proclamation was issued by the President of the United States, containing, among other things, the following, to wit:

"That on the first day of January, in the year of our Lord one thousand eight hundred and sixty-three, all persons held as slaves within any State, or designated part of a State, the people whereof shall then be in rebellion against the United States, shall be then, thenceforward, and forever free; and the Executive Government of the United States, including the military and naval authority thereof, will recognize and maintain the freedom of such persons, and will do no act or acts to repress such persons, or any of them, in any efforts they may make for their actual freedom.

"That the Executive will, on the first day of January aforesaid, by proclamation, designate the States and parts of States, if any, in which the people thereof respectively shall then be in rebellion against the United States; and the fact that any State, or the people thereof, shall on that day be in good faith represented in the Congress of the United States by members chosen thereto at elections wherein a majority of the qualified voters of such State shall have participated, shall in the absence of strong countervailing testimony be deemed conclusive evidence that such State and the people thereof are not then in rebellion against the United States."

Now, therefore, I, Abraham Lincoln, President of the United States, by virtue of the power in me vested as commander-in-chief of the army and navy of the United States, in time of actual armed rebellion against the authority and government of the United States, and as a fit and necessary war measure for suppressing said rebellion, do, on this first day of January, in the year of our Lord one thousand eight hundred and sixty-three, and in accordance with my purpose so to do, publicly proclaimed for the full period of 100 days from the day first above mentioned, order and designate as the States and parts of States wherein

171

the people thereof, respectively, are this day in rebellion against the United States, the following, to wit:

Arkansas, Texas, Louisiana (except the parishes of St. Bernard, Plaquemines, Jefferson, St. John, St. Charles, St. James, Ascension, Assumption, Terre Bonne, Lafourche, St. Mary, St. Martin, and Orleans, including the city of New Orleans), Mississippi, Alabama, Florida, Georgia, South Carolina, North Carolina, and Virginia (except the forty-eight counties designated as West Virginia and also the counties of Berkeley, Accomac, Northampton, Elizabeth City, York, Princess Ann, and Norfolk, including the cities of Norfolk and Portsmouth), and which excepted parts are for the present left precisely as if this proclamation were not issued.

And by virtue of the power and for the purpose aforesaid, I do order and declare that all persons held as slaves within said designated States and parts of States are, and henceforward shall be, free; and that the Executive Government of the United States, including the military and naval authorities thereof, will recognize and maintain the freedom of said persons.

And I hereby enjoin upon the people so declared to be free to abstain from all violence, unless in necessary self-defense; and I recommend to them that, in all cases when allowed, they labor faithfully for reasonable wages.

And I further declare and make known that such persons of suitable condition will be received into the armed service of the United States to garrison forts, positions, stations, and other places, and to man vessels of all sorts in said service.

And upon this act, sincerely believed to be an act of justice, warranted by the Constitution upon military necessity, I invoke the considerate judgment of mankind and the gracious favor of Almighty God.

In witness whereof, I have hereunto set my hand, and caused the seal of the United States to be affixed.

Done at the city of Washington, this first day of January, in the year of our Lord one thousand eight hundred and sixty-three, and of the independence of the United States of America the eighty-seventh.

ABRAHAM LINCOLN.

By the President: William H. Seward, Secretary of State.

INDEX

Abolitionists, the, 39, 48-50, 82, 88, 139
Adams, Charles Francis, 81
Adams, John, 32
Adams, John Quincy, 77
Alamo, the, 79-80
Amiens, peace of, 33
Anderson, Major Robert, 129
Andrew, John A., 81, 150
Anne, Queen, 20
Antietam, battle of, 156
Appomattox, 166, 167
Atlantic cable, the, 162

Bancroft, George, 139
Bates, Edward, 115
Bell, John, 108
Benton, Thomas H., 77
Berkeley, Governor, 20
Beveridge, Senator Albert J., 74
Blair, Montgomery, 115, 154, 168
Brazil, slavery in, 40
Breckenridge, John C., 106
Brissot, 26, 32
Brown, Rev. George, 49
Brown, John, 88, 104
Buchanan, James, 98, 99, 109, 110, 111, 113, 120, 121, 129
Bull Run, first battle of, 135; second battle of, 148
Burnside, General, 160
Busey, Dr. Samuel, 78-79
Butler, General Benjamin F., 136, 137, 143-144

Calhoun, John, 77
California, the gold rush to, 87;
admitted to the Union as a free state, 87
Cameron, Simon, 114
Canada, slavery in, 27, 28
Carlyle, Thomas, 48
Carolinas, the, early slavery in, 20-21
Carroll, Charles, of Carrollton, 30
Cartwright, Edmund, invention of power loom, 35
Cartwright, Rev. Peter, candidate for Congress, against Lincoln, 76, 91
Cass, Lewis, 64, 77
Channing, 41
Charles II of England, 20, 21
Charleston, South Carolina, 36, 44
Chase, Salmon P., 114-115, 128, 133, 154, 156, 160
Chevalier, Michael, 42, 45-46
Christianity and slavery, 14
Civil War, the: the first signs of disunion, 38ff.; slavery becoming the great national issue, 84ff.; the election of 1860 and the secession of the Southern States, 106-113; war precipitated by the firing on Fort Sumter, 134; the character of the war, 134-135; a résumé of the course of the war, 135-149, 160, 161-162, 164-166
Clarkson, Thomas, 26
Clay, Henry, 50, 81
Cobb, Senator Thomas, 112
Columbus, Christopher, 17
Compromise of 1850, the, 50, 84

Condorcet, 26
Connecticut, emancipation in, 32
Constitutional Union party, the, 108
Cooper, Dr. Thomas, 48
Cotton, 35-37
Cowper, William, 25
Crittenden, John J., 77
Cuba, 40

Davis, Jefferson, 80, 89, 143, 155
Declaration of Independence, the, 26, 28
Delaware, failure of abolition in, 32
Democratic party, the, and slavery, 38, 50
Dew, Professor Thomas, 48
Dickens, Charles, 40-42, 58, 69, 77-78, 157
District of Columbia, compensated abolition in, 147
Dix, General John A., 110-111, 133, 138
Donelson, Fort, 142
Douglas, Stephen A., 69, 77, 84, 88, 90, 96, 97, 99-100, 101-104, 106, 120-121
Douglass, Frederick, 49
Dred Scott decision, the, 89, 98-99
Dutch East Indies, slavery in, 39, 40

Elizabeth, Queen, 15, 16
Emancipation Proclamation, the, 153-160; some reactions to the Proclamation, 162-163; the final draft, 171-172
England, the part taken by the British in the slave-trade, 21-22; the outlawing of the slave-trade by, 25-26; abolition of slavery in its colonies, 39

Farragut, Admiral, 143
Ferdinand, King, 18
Foster, Rev. Stephen, 49
Fox, Captain Gustavus, 130
France, abolition of slavery in its colonies, 39
Fredericksburg, battle of, 160
Free Soil party, the, 81
Frémont, General John C., 98, 99, 138
Fugitive Slave Law, the, 50, 84-85

Gadsden, James, 31
Garrison, William Lloyd, 49, 139
George III of England, 26, 31
Georgia, slavery at first forbidden in the colony, 21; slavery introduced in, 27
Gettysburg, battle of, 161
Ghent, Treaty of, 33
Gilmer, John A., 115
Grant, General, 142-143, 166, 167
Great Britain, see England
Greeley, Horace, 152

Hall, Captain Basil, 42, 43-44
Halleck, General, 138
Hartney, David, 25
Hawkins, Sir John, 16, 21
Hawks, John, kinsman of Lincoln, 62
Hay, John, 29, 95, 102, 113, 114, 118, 120, 131, 145, 147, 156, 164
Henry, Fort, 142
Henry, Patrick, 112
Herndon, "Billy," law partner and biographer of Lincoln, 70, 71, 73, 83, 91, 94, 95, 121, 131
Hill, B. H., 112
Hill, John, 49
Hispaniola, 18
Houston, Samuel, 112
Hunter, General David, 144-145

Illinois, as the storm center of the United States in the politics of the 1850's, 89-90

Immigration to America, 33, 34

Indians, not adaptable as slaves, 17-18; true character of, 18, 25

Industrial revolution, the, 33

Isabella, Queen, 17

Jackson, Andrew, 66, 110

Jackson, "Stonewall," 148

Jamaica, numbers of slaves brought to, 22

Jefferson, Thomas, 31, 38, 86, 112

Johnson, Andrew, 168

Johnson, Doctor, 25

Johnston, General Joseph E., 147, 167

Kansas-Nebraska disturbances, the, 86-89, 96

Kellogg, Congressman, of Illinois, 117

Lafayette, 26, 32, 40

Las Casas, 18

Laurens, Henry, 31

Lecky, the historian, 23

Lee, General, 148, 155-156, 161; his surrender, 166, 167-168

Letcher, Governor, of Virginia, 113

Lincoln, Abraham, 29, 34, 39, 40, 50; his person and strength, 51, 60; the myth of history regarding the man, and the truth as to his capacity and character, 51-55; the frontier environment of his boyhood, 55-58; death of his mother, 58-59; his childhood and youth, 59-63; visit to New Orleans in 1831 and the result on his opinion on slavery, 61-62; early failures in business at New Salem, Illinois, 63, 64, 68; in the Black Hawk War, 63-64; first term in the Illinois legislature, 65-67; the dilemma in his mind on slavery, 67; courtship of Anne Rutledge and her death, 67-68; reëlection to the legislature, 68; removal to Springfield and practice of law there, 68ff.; the Lincoln stories, 70-71; the tragedy of his marriage to Mary Todd, 71-74; his children, 74; service in the legislature till 1843, 74-75; term in Congress, 75-82; his Mexican War speech and its results, 79-80; the academic case for secession, 80; in the presidential campaign of 1848, 81-82; denunciation of Abolitionists, 82; proposal as to slavery in the District of Columbia, 82; return to the practice of law at Springfield, 83, 90; meeting with Mrs. Stowe, 86; return to politics in 1854, 89, 91, 95ff.; his reputation for honesty, 90-91; his religious opinions and beliefs, 91-95; the change in his character and views, 91, 95, 96; utterance on slavery in the campaign of 1854, 96-97; his rise as a national figure, 97, 98-99, 104-105; unsuccessful candidacy for the Senate in 1858 and development of his argument on slavery, 99-104; the Lincoln-Douglas debates, 101-104; the Cooper Union speech, 104-105; nomination and election as President in 1860, 105-109; selection of his cabinet, 114-115; his views as shown by his correspondence before his inauguration, 115-

Lincoln, Abraham (*Continued*) 117; the journey to Washington and the Inaugural Address, 117-125; the indecision and inaction of the first few months of his administration, 126-134; calls for 75,000 militia after the fall of Sumter, 135; plan of compensated abolition, 140, 146-147, 151; arrival at the conviction that the slaves must be freed, 149-152; his famous public letter to Greeley, 151-152; the first reading of the Emancipation Proclamation to his cabinet, 153-155; the publication of the Proclamation after Antietam and its final drafting, 156-160; the change in himself after the issue of the Proclamation, 163-164; his forestalling the vengeance of the politicians on the South, 167; assassination of, 169-170

Lincoln, Sarah, step-mother of Abraham Lincoln, 59

Lincoln, Thomas, father of Abraham Lincoln, 55, 57, 58, 59, 61

Logan, Judge, law partner of Lincoln, 70

Longfellow, 29, 41, 81

Louisiana Purchase, the, 37

Lovejoy, Rev. Elijah P., the abolitionist, killing of, 74, 82

Lowell, James Russell, 81

Lucretius, 14

Lyell, Sir Charles, 42, 43

McBride, Judge, 167, 168

McClellan, General George B., 80, 135-140, 147-148, 155-156

Macaulay, Zachary, 26

Mackay, Alexander, 43

Magruder, General John B., 137, 139

Mansfield, Lord, 25, 27

Mark Twain, 29, 47, 93

Marryatt, Captain, 42, 44

Martineau, Harriet, 42, 44-45

Maryland, failure of abolition in, 32

Massachusetts, end of slavery in, 28, 32

Meade, General, 161

Mexican War, the, 39, 79-80

Mexico, abolition of slavery in, 39

Middle Ages, character of the people of the, 16

Milton, John, 25

"Missouri Compromise," the, 38, 87; repeal of, 88

More, Thomas, 14

Moultrie, General, 36

Napoleon I, 34

Napoleon III, 75

New England in the slave-trade, 21

New Jersey, emancipation in, 32

New Orleans, capture of, 143

New York State, emancipation in, 32

Nicolay, John, 95, 114

Nicolay and Hay, *Complete Works* of Lincoln, edited by, 102

Oglethorpe, General James, 21

Olmstead, Frederick, 30

Owen, Robert, 60-61

Owens, Mary, Lincoln's engagement to, 68

Palmerston, Lord, 141

Parker, Theodore, 49

Pennsylvania, emancipation in, 32

Phillips, Wendell, 49, 82, 139

Pierce, Franklin, 89
Pinkerton, Allan, 119
Pitt, William, 32
Pope, Alexander, 25
Pope, General, 148
Port Royal, capture of, 144
Portugal, abolition of slavery in its colonies, 39
Presidential campaign of 1856, 97-98; of 1860, 105-106, 107-109

Quakers, the, 25

Religious persecution, 23-24
Republican party, the, 90; national organization in 1856, 97-98
Rhode Island, emancipation in, 32
Rhodes, Cecil, 21
Rhodes, James, the historian, 128, 133, 143
Rice, 20, 37
Rolfe, John, 19
Roosevelt, Theodore, 114
Rousseau, 25, 32
Royal African (Slave) Company, the, 20, 21
Rutledge, Anne, 67-68, 72

San Domingo, the slave insurrection in, 26
Santa Anna, 79
Schouler, the historian, 124
Scott, General Winfield, 119, 120, 126, 136
Serfdom in Europe, 39
Seward, William H., 105, 106, 114, 116, 122, 124, 128, 131, 133, 142, 153, 154-155, 159
Sharp, Granville, 26
Sherman, General, 138, 144, 164-165, 167
Shiloh, battle of, 143

Slavery, general attitude of the American people toward, while it existed, 13-14, 27-28; in ancient times, 14; dies out in Europe for economic reasons, 15; brought to life again incident to the colonization of the New World, 15-18; beginnings of the African slave trade, 18-19; the introduction of slavery into the English colonies in America, 19-21; the part taken by the British in the slave-trade, 21-22; number of slaves brought from Africa in the eighteenth century, 22; the horrors of the trade, 22-24; beginnings of opposition to the traffic, 24-25; the outlawing of the slave-trade, 26; the status of slavery in America at this period, 27-28; signs of the passing of the institution in the United States, both for economic and moral reasons, 28-31; abolition of slavery in the Northern States, 28, 32; slavery kept out of the Northwest Territory, 34; rooted to the soil in the South, 34-35, 37; the "Missouri Compromise," and the first signs of the disunion sentiment, 38ff.; abolition by various nations, 39; contemporary judgments before the Civil War on American slavery, 40-48; Southern arguments in its defense, 48; assaults of the abolitionists on the institution, 48-50; the slavery compromise of 1850, 50, 84; slavery becoming the great national issue, 84ff.; the "underground railway," 85; the effect of *Uncle Tom's Cabin* on sentiment, 85-86; the Kansas-Ne-

Slavery (*Continued*)
  braska struggle, 86-89, 96; the
  Dred Scott decision, 89, 98-99;
  Lincoln's utterance, on slavery
  after 1854, 96-97, 100-101, 103,
  104-105; attitude of the political parties on slavery in the
  election of 1860, 107-109; the
  indefinite status of slavery during the first months of the Civil
  War, 136-140, 144-147; the un-
  founded fear of a slave uprising,
  46-47, 136-137, 166-167; Lincoln's plan of compensated
  abolition, 140, 146-147, 151;
  the Emancipation Proclamation,
  153-160
Smith, Adam, 25, 32
Smith, Caleb, 115
Smith, Goldwin, 119
South Carolina, early secession
  sentiment in, 66; the first State
  to secede, 106
Springfield, Illinois, 58, 69, 90
"Squatter sovereignty," the doc-
  trine of, 88, 99-100
Stanton, Edwin, 129, 153, 154, 156,
  157, 168
Stephens, Alexander H., 77, 112
Stowe, Harriet Beecher, 85-86
Stuart, John T., Lincoln's law
  partnership with, 69, 70, 94
Sugar, 37
Sumner, Charles, 81
Sumter, Fort, 129-130, 131, 134

Taney, Chief Justice Roger B., 89,
  99, 120, 121-122
Taylor, Zachary, 80, 81, 82
Texas, annexation of, 39

Thomson, James, 25
Times, the London, 162-163
Tobacco, 19-20, 37
Todd, Mary, her marriage to
  Lincoln, 71-73
Toombs, Robert, 77
Trent affair, the, 140-142
Trollope, Mrs., 42
Turner, Nat, slave uprising led
  by, 49

Uncle Tom's Cabin, 85-86
"Underground railway," the, 85
Utrecht, Treaty of, 22

Vicksburg, fall of, 161
Vienna, Congress of, 26
Virginia, early slavery in, 19-20,
  22; business of raising slaves in,
  for sale in other Southern
  states, 37

Walker, General Francis, 166
Ward, Artemus, 132, 156, 157-158
Washington, George, 28, 29, 30,
  31, 112
Washington, the city of, in 1847,
  77-78
Waterloo, battle of, 33
Webster, Daniel, 50, 77
Welles, Gideon, 115, 150, 153, 159
West Virginia made a separate
  State during the Civil War, 135
Whig party, the, and slavery, 38,
  50; the end of the party in 1856,
  97
Whitney, Eli, and the cotton gin,
  35, 36
Whittier, John G., 81
Wilberforce, William, 26
William and Mary of England, 21